LeMond

LeMond

The Incredible Comeback of an American Hero

SAMUEL ABT

RANDOM HOUSE
NEW YORK

Library of Congress Cataloging-in-Publication Data

Abt, Samuel.
LeMond: the incredible comeback of an American hero / by Samuel Abt.
p.cm.
ISBN 0-394-58476-7
1. LeMond, Greg.   2. Cyclists—United States—Biography.   3. Tour
de France (Bicycle race) I. Title.
GV1051.L45A65   1990
796.6'092—dc20
[B]   89-43428

Manufactured in the United States of America
98765432
First Edition
Book design by Jo Anne Metsch

This book is for Vicki and Irv.

The difference between a successful
person and others is not a lack of strength,
not a lack of knowledge, but rather a
lack of will.

—Vince Lombardi

When you ain't got nothing, you got
nothing to lose.

—Bob Dylan

ACKNOWLEDGMENTS

For their editorial support, I owe thanks to Theodore Costantino and Christopher Koch of *Bicycle Guide* magazine, to Joseph Vecchione and his fine editors at *The New York Times*, to George Downing, and to Ed Victor, my agent.

On the road, for sharing and good times, I owe thanks to Robert Zeller, Pierre Hamel, Phil Liggett, Geoffrey Nicholson, Stephen Bierley, Keith Bingham, Salvatore Zanca, Mike Price, and John Wilcockson.

Greg, Kathy, Bob, and Bertha LeMond deserve special gratitude for their cooperation and friendship over the years.

And once more, with love and respect, I thank my children, Claire, Phoebe, and John, for caring and for making that caring evident.

CONTENTS

LeMond

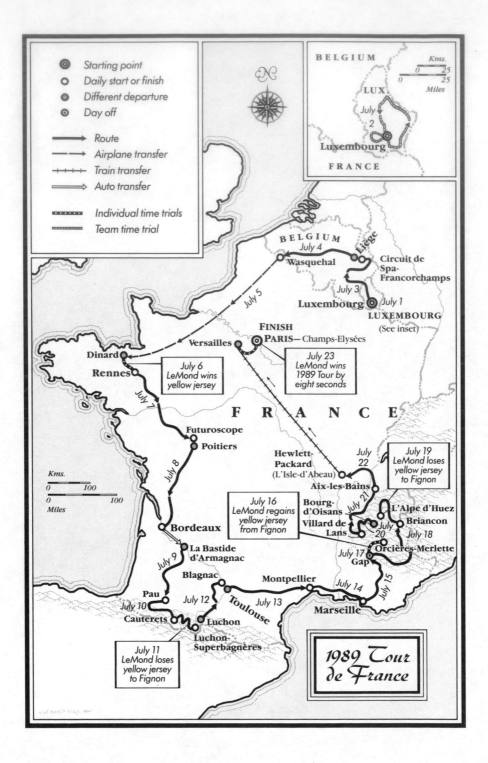

Starting point
Daily start or finish
Different departure
Day off

Route
Airplane transfer
Train transfer
Auto transfer

Individual time trials
Team time trial

BELGIUM

LUX

July
2

Luxembourg

FRANCE

Kms.
0   25
0   25
Miles

BELGIUM

Liège
July 4

Wasquehal

Circuit de
Spa-
Francorchamps

July 3

July 5

Luxembourg   July 1

LUXEMBOURG
(See inset)

FINISH
PARIS— Champs-Elysées

Versailles

Dinard

Rennes

July 6
LeMond wins
yellow jersey

July 23
LeMond wins
1989 Tour by
eight seconds

F R A N C E

July 7

Futuroscope
Poitiers

Hewlett-
Packard
(L'Isle-d'Abeau)

July
22

July 19
LeMond loses
yellow jersey
to Fignon

Kms.
0   100
0   100
Miles

July 8

Aix-les-Bains

July 21

July 16
LeMond regains
yellow jersey
from Fignon

Bourg-
d'Oisans
Villard de
Lans

L'Alpe d'Huez
Briançon

July 18

Bordeaux

La Bastide
d'Armagnac

July
20

Orcières-Merlette

July 17

Gap

July 9

Blagnac

Montpellier

July 14

July 15

Pau

July 10

July 12

Toulouse

July 13

Marseille

Cauterets

Luchon

Luchon-
Superbagnères

July 11
LeMond loses
yellow jersey
to Fignon

*1989 Tour
de France*

1

The Sun King Storms Paris

Greg LeMond was weeping. Still wearing the sweat-soaked jersey he had worn that day in the Giro d'Italia, he sat on his bed in a shabby hotel and cried in rage and frustration. Acclaimed only two years before as the strongest bicycle racer of his time, he had lost his power. His body was betraying him almost daily in the three-week-long race. Where he wanted to ride was at the front of the pack, where the champions rode, but at each climb he slipped slowly back toward the rear to join the unknowns and second-raters who straggled to the finish line long after the leaders had crossed it. They were a sad lot, the riders at the back of the race, and when they finally made it to the finish, nobody wanted to look them in the face or crack a small joke. How do you console a man for his lack of talent? Worse, what words or gestures can comfort a fallen champion? So, this evening late in May 1989, Greg LeMond sat on his bed and wept.

HE RODE THE perfect ride, the fastest any man has raced in the history of the Tour de France, and now Greg LeMond was standing in the middle of the Champs-Elysées and waiting to find out whether the ride had been perfect enough. His jersey unzipped to help him cool off, a huge bottle of water in his left hand, LeMond watched the clock. Across the broad avenue, another rider, Laurent Fignon, labored uphill toward the Arc de Triomphe as loudspeakers ticked off the seconds. Fignon made his turn and began the descent toward LeMond, but by then it was too late: time had run out. After three weeks and 2,025 miles, the American was first by a mere eight seconds.

LeMond had just won the Tour de France for the second time, and half a million people lining the Champs-Elysées were cheering him and chanting his name. Fans unfurled the American flag, and the light breeze of this summer day spread its colors as a French military band broke into "The Star-Spangled Banner." Not many years before, an American would have been as unlikely to win the Tour de France as a Frenchman would be to pitch a no-hitter in the World Series. No non-European had ever won the race before LeMond. Wearing a huge grin, he waved to the crowd in triumph. His smile was joyous, but his thoughts were bittersweet, nearly somber. "Only a month and a half ago, I thought I was ready to quit cycling," he admitted later.

The road to the victory podium in Paris had been a long one. More than two years before, LeMond had been shot and nearly killed in a hunting accident, and now his happiness was mixed with memories of his pain. The boyish, roughly handsome LeMond frowned and his blue eyes narrowed when he thought about his recovery. And now he was on top again.

"The key is being able to endure psychologically," LeMond explained. "When you're not riding well, you think, Why suffer? Why push yourself for four or five hours? The mountains are the pinnacle of suffering. You don't know when you're going to explode, when you have to back off. You're pushing yourself almost to your maximum; then you recuperate and do it again. You might do it ten or fifteen times in a race. When you don't have the conditioning or if you've been away from it a long time, you forget how much cycling hurts. You really forget."

Yet the two summers he had been forced to miss the Tour de France had not been enjoyable. "I figure I've got a natural talent, and I want to make the most of it," he said. He was obsessed by the desire to win the world's greatest bicycle race again, to prove that he was the best, to stand on the podium on the Champs-Elysées hearing his name chanted by half a million people, and to wave back at them in triumph.

He was the Sun King, as a French newspaper christened him. This was not just because of the bright yellow jersey that LeMond was pulling over his head now to signify that he was the Tour de France's leader. The yellow jersey is awarded after each daily stage but the most glorious one to win is the one LeMond was donning—the final yellow jersey, the yellow jersey of the race's winner. Nor was he the Sun King because of the route he had just traveled into Paris, though this began in Versailles with the royal palace as a backdrop. It was not even because of the radiance of LeMond's smile as he held his son Geoffrey in his arms and beamed at his subjects. It was not any one of these, and yet it was all of them.

Louis XIV won the nickname of the Sun King for the grandeur of his reign and for the way he made the nobility dance attendance on him. "L'état, c'est moi," he could say, and he was right: he *was* the state. Now, in this bicentennial year of the French Revolution, LeMond could say it too.

While loudspeakers along the avenue announced his victory, the cheers moved like a wave from the Place de la Concorde up to the Arc de Triomphe and back again on the eerily empty thoroughfare. Only twice a year is the Champs-Elysées closed to traffic: on July 14 for the traditional military parade that marks the fall of the Bastille, and for the finish of the Tour de France, so important is the race to the French public. Under a bright sky and hot sun, tourists who had planned to spend this Sunday strolling along the avenue, admiring its gift shops and sidewalk cafés, found themselves barely able to slip through the spectators packed six and seven deep behind steel barricades.

Only a few thousand of the assembled half million could see LeMond, who was pumping his arms in triumph as he grinned disbelievingly. His eight-second victory was the smallest in the bicycle race's eighty-six-year history, but this was only a minor part of the drama. Twenty-seven months before he had been lying in a field in northern California, shot accidentally by his brother-in-law. "The doctor said I was within twenty minutes of bleeding to death." Ravaged by pain and weakness, LeMond needed two years to rebuild his body. He still carried two buckshot pellets in the lining of his heart.

Now LeMond was jubilant. "Unbelievable, just unbelievable," he kept repeating, brimming with victory, as he exuberantly hugged his wife. While the police cleared his way, he mounted the steps of the platform to greet officials of the race and of the French government and diplomatic corps. All of them hurried over to shake his hand and to jostle for a place in the pictures being taken by the swarm of photographers crouched below the podium. "Greg, Greg," they shouted to get his attention for a full-face photograph. They needn't have bothered: he continued to swivel, dazed with victory and happiness, looking up and down the avenue. Television cameras took in the long line of plane trees and horse chestnuts, the Obelisk in the nearby Place de la Concorde, the Louvre a smudge behind the Tuileries Gardens, the Grand and Petit Palais, and finally the Arc de Triomphe. The photographs would be on the front pages of newspapers around the world the next morning, and live television coverage was being beamed throughout Europe, North and South America, and parts of Africa and Asia.

LeMond looked ecstatic and so did his son, wearing the fluorescent pink cap of his father's American team. The last time Geoffrey had mounted the victory podium at the end of the Tour de France, he had been two years old, and petrified. "All those people, all that noise," his mother, Kathy, said. "It was even worse when we left the podium. If Greg just turned his head or his body, the police would smash whoever was in that direction."

The crowd control was better this time and Geoffrey, now five, waved from his father's arms. To avoid traumatizing the LeMonds' second son, two-year-old Scott, Kathy had him sit with his grandparents in the nearby bleachers. "If Greg wins every time one of our children is two years old, he ought to be first again in 1991," Kathy joked, referring to her pregnancy, then in its sixth month.

The entire family—parents, grandparents, and small children—was in a joking mood. LeMond's mother, father, and wife had spent the last week of the race with him, keeping him company as the pressure rose, looking after his interests, and cheering him on. The LeMonds are an extremely close family.

"I think Greg's family is the most important thing in his career, without a doubt," Kathy said during the race. "Without that stability, he might never have gotten where he is now—certainly not without his parents at the very beginning. They're incredible." Greg's parents, she said, had been completely supportive: "Whatever Greg says, goes."

Alone later, in the Alps one day in the Tour, sitting on a massage table in a T-shirt and with a towel knotted around his middle, LeMond considered a question about how important his family had been to his comeback, and how much of his recovery he owed to his wife and children. "How do you put a value on that?" he asked slowly, looking out the window at the Alps. "How do you say how much you owe?" Then he answered his own question. "For me, there's no purpose if you don't have a wife and kids; there's really no purpose to make money or be successful. I can't imagine being single and working so hard. I've been criticized by some of the European press for being businesslike, and I'm that way because I realize my value to a sponsor. But mostly I do it because I have a family. If I were single, I'd take things a lot easier. I'm racing and making a lot of sacrifices for my family, making sure we're going to have a nice life when I'm done with cycling. Without them, I know I wouldn't be nearly this successful."

Still, LeMond continued, looking at the ceiling as if searching for words, he owed a special debt to his parents. "They're the foundation for my cycling," he said firmly. "There's no way to place a value on them. They were incredibly supportive when I started cycling, and they still are. Without my dad . . ."

Now, in Paris, after he picked up a check for 1.5 million francs (then about $250,000) for his victory and finished talking to television interviewers, LeMond and his family returned to their hotel and posed happily for more photographers. Then LeMond went to a nearby fast-food restaurant for the hamburger that he had promised to treat himself to after the three-week race. Later the children were parked with a baby-sitter and the family went nightclubbing to celebrate. A photo of the wanly smiling LeMond flanked by Moulin Rouge showgirls wearing flimsy costumes and cellophane grins made the front page of the afternoon newspapers. By their standards LeMond and his wife left early; in 1986, to celebrate his first Tour de France triumph, they stayed out till five A.M. This time they left at midnight, returned to the Champs-Elysées for ice cream, and then went back to their hotel for more talk and, finally, sleep.

Predictably, the newspaper and magazine stories the next week were all the same. It was not that at the age of twenty-eight LeMond had won the Tour de France for the second time. Other riders had done that, and three of them had won it five times. What made LeMond so special was how long and difficult the road back to the victory podium had been.

What was going through his head as the military band played his national anthem? He was remembering the shooting, and the emergency appendectomy a few months later that ended whatever hopes he had of salvaging the 1987 season. He was thinking of 1988, when he developed shin tendinitis that finally forced an operation and kept him out of the Tour for a second successive year. It was a bitter summer that he recalled, not the sweet summer that his wife remembered.

"Nineteen eighty-eight was the best summer of our lives," Kathy said. "Greg had a cast because of his operation, so he went fishing because he couldn't ride his bike, and he spent the whole day with me and the kids." The LeMonds have a big house on Lake Minnetonka in Wayzata, near Minneapolis, and they split the year between it and the house they occupy in Belgium during the racing season. "We said, 'This is what life is like when you're not doing the Tour de France.' We agreed that it was the best summer of our lives. But for now, racing is what he really wants to do. We can always do the other again in four or five years."

LeMond agreed completely. "We had a great time last summer," he said, breaking into a smile of pleasure. Did he wish that he was back in Minnesota at this moment? "No, no," he said hurriedly. "I'd much rather be here. I love the Tour. I know I'd regret it if I didn't put out a hundred percent in this sport. I feel I have put out a hundred percent the last two years.

"In these years I've noticed a kind of sly smile on a lot of people's faces, a kind of happiness that some people had. It was as if they were saying, 'See, I told you he'd never come back.' The best thing about all this is that I have the last say."

In 1978, when he was just short of seventeen years old, Greg LeMond sat in his bedroom in the Washoe Valley of Nevada, halfway between Reno and Carson City, and on a yellow pad wrote down his goals. Years later, he ticked them off one by one on his fingers.

"I wanted to accomplish something by the time I was twenty-four or twenty-five. What I didn't want was to be the kind of cyclist who just stuck it out and stayed in the sport for ten years without being successful. So I sat down before the junior world championships and wrote for 1978: 'Place well for experience in junior world championships.' Then I wrote that in 1979 I want to win the junior worlds. The following year I wanted to win the Olympic road race. By the time I was twenty-two or twenty-three I wanted to win the professional world championship, and by the time I was twenty-four or twenty-five I wanted to win the Tour de France.

"I actually wrote all this down," LeMond continued. "I don't know where the list is now, but I think I still have it somewhere. I was almost seventeen years old and I was determined that this was the way I wanted my career to go. What's amazing is that it's just the way it went. Everything that was on that paper I did—except for the Olympics, because that was the year of the United States boycott."

By far the biggest triumph on that list was LeMond's winning the Tour de France in 1986, the year before he was shot. "There's no race like the Tour," LeMond often says, and he is right. In financial rewards, and especially in respect, the Tour de France is the jewel of professional bicycling. As an American once wrote in trying to explain the sport to other Americans, imagine the World Series and the Super Bowl rolled into one event; then imagine this event lasting three weeks and traveling around the country while being watched live by twenty million people.

On his first trip to Europe in 1978, LeMond met a boyhood hero, Jean-Claude Killy, the winner of three gold medals in skiing at the 1968 Olympic Games in Grenoble, France. They went bicycling near the ski resort of Morzine in France just as the Tour de France was going by. "It was my first sight of professional racers," LeMond remembered. "I won't even pretend that I thought to myself, Someday I'll be riding in the Tour on that road, but sure enough, in 1984 I did."

LeMond was amazed by his first sight of the race. "I was awed by how many people were watching—a couple of hundred thousand spread along the course—and by how fit the riders were. They were like gods. I also couldn't believe how hard it seemed. But of course I was looking at it through the eyes of somebody who practiced the sport and could understand its difficulties. From experience I knew how the pain of cycling can be terrible: in your legs, your chest, everywhere. You go into oxygen debt and fall apart. Not many people outside cycling understand that, and a decade ago they tended to underestimate cycling—if they paid any attention to it at all. Early in my career, I was embarrassed to say I was a bike rider. 'I'm a bike rider.' 'Oh, you're one of the guys who race motorcycles.' I'd always have to explain that cycling is one of the most popular sports in the world. If the average person tried professional cycling, he'd say, 'My God, I can't believe how tough this is.' Everybody says how hard a marathon is, but twenty five thousand people show up for one in New York. Only two hundred people can enter the Tour de France, and it takes years to get there because you can't just sign yourself up for it.

"I'm not just talking about being recognized by the public. I believe that cycling is the toughest sport of all, and if I'm at the top of what's at least one of the toughest sports, then I've got to be one of the top American athletes. That's the kind of respect an athlete likes—to be respected by other athletes.''

This was the new Sun King speaking. As the French public cheered him and newspaper editors around the world once again put his photograph on page one, many earlier and un-happier years were forgotten: the fights with employers over broken agreements; the controversial $1 million contract he signed late in 1984, which shattered the salary scale in the sport; his feud with Bernard Hinault, once his idol and mentor, over who would win the 1986 Tour. Greg LeMond had waged a long fight to get to the top, not once but twice. If he was young, rich, famous, and dazzling in victory, his life had not been easy. For the last two years especially, it had been uphill all the way.

2

A Winner from the Start

*The salesman was trying hard to steer the fourteen-year-old boy
away from his choice of a bicycle. Yes, it was a fine value for its
price, and yes, it was a good fit too. But the color! Bright yellow,
the bicycle practically shrieked at you. Greg LeMond knew what
he wanted, though; on a bright yellow bicycle, a rider would have
to be noticed. Nobody could miss him when he cruised first across
the finish line and shot a fist into the air, the way riders were
photographed in fan magazines. Just to make sure he would be
noticed, the boy chose a yellow jersey to go with the bicycle. At his
side, smiling indulgently and, as always, trusting his son's
judgment, Bob LeMond was happy to pay for the bicycle and
jersey. Now they were ready for Greg's first race.*

KENT GORDIS WAS feeling cocky, and why not? A member of
the Velo Sport Berkeley Club in California in 1976, fourteen-
year-old Gordis had spent the winter training with George

Mount, one of the first American cyclists to have raced in Europe and now a big name in the sport back home. "I was the only one in the club to keep up with George, so I felt I would be by far the best intermediate racer," Gordis said many years later. "Frankly, I was pretty sure of myself. Then I met Greg." Gordis, now a television producer who specializes in bicycling coverage, remembers well that minor race in California when the two of them were fourteen years old. "Greg and I started racing the same day, the same race."

Gordis's voice turned affectionate "The race starts and LeMond breaks away," he said. "I could barely hold his wheel, and at the finish he beat me by eleven or twelve lengths. I was second and the third rider was ten minutes behind."

Born on the same day, June 26, 1961, Gordis and LeMond became fast friends and have remained close through the years. "From the start we hit it off," Gordis said. As boys, they often spent time at each other's homes, and when LeMond visited Europe for the first time, he went with the Gordis family. "The good Greg we know now—friendly, warm, outgoing, what the French call *sympa*, not affected—was always that way," Gordis said. Today he is a big man, weighing nearly two hundred pounds, and could be considered out of shape even for a television producer, but as he talked about the 1976 race, he sketched a picture of two trim, athletic boys eager to prove how good they were.

Trim? With a laugh, Gordis recalled LeMond through the eyes of a rival. "He was this skinny kid, and he wore a ridiculous canary-yellow jersey and had a canary-yellow bike. I took one look at him and bent over in derision." The jersey and bicycle were LeMond's pride and joy. "I was feeling cocky," Gordis continued. "I had stayed with George Mount up in the hills. How could a skinny kid in a canary-yellow jersey possibly beat me?" he asked rhetorically. "Afterward I was really depressed that 'the turkey,' as I called him, had beat me by eleven or twelve lengths. If the turkey had beat me, how could I possibly be any good?" In fact, burdened by sinus trouble and by his big frame, Gordis switched from bicycling to hockey when he enrolled at Yale a few years later. Now he jokingly denied that LeMond's victory in that first race had ruined his morale.

" 'The turkey,' " he repeated, shaking his head in disbelief. "My judgment was a little off. Right there, right at the very beginning, it was obvious that Greg was simply an outstanding athlete, an unbelievably outstanding athlete."

So he was, and so he is. LeMond came to bicycling by way of downhill skiing, which he began before the age of eight when his parents moved from his birthplace in Lakewood, California, outside Los Angeles, to Lake Tahoe, California. The family lived in Lake Tahoe for three years and then, because of his father's prospering career as a real-estate broker, moved to Nevada, settling in ranch country in the Washoe Valley.

For a young athlete it was ideal country, broad and open under the blazing sun of summer and the heavy snows of winter. LeMond began hunting and then trapshooting, a sport his parents, Bob and Bertha, both practiced, a year or two before reaching his teens. "Since we lived way out in the country," he remembered, "hunting and trapshooting were something to do outdoors. I also went backpacking almost every weekend when I was thirteen and fourteen. At one point I was so into it that I bought all these books about it, like *The Complete Walker*, and read them over and over again. Before I ever got involved in cycling, I had planned to spend the following summer—that would have been 1975—walking the Muir Trail from Canada to Mexico, or at least parts of it. It would have been a one- or two-month backpack to stay in shape for skiing. I did a lot of backpacking each summer weekend just before I got involved in cycling and it helped me keep in condition.

"And fishing, fly-fishing. There was a small stream up behind our house, with brook trout. I taught myself how to fly-fish—I learned by practicing on the brook trout—and got to be pretty good at it. My dad didn't fish with me but we did a lot of target shooting together once a week. I really liked the sport and lifted bricks to build my arm strength so I could hold the gun up. When you shoot a hundred targets, it takes quite a bit of arm power. It's funny to have started on the way to cycling like that because none of the muscles or reflexes you develop in target shooting or fishing help you at all on a bicycle. But those sports were one of the reasons I got into cycling. Since we lived out in the country, I was never close enough to school to participate in team sports. I went to school by bus, sometimes an hour each way. Sure, I played football during recess, and baseball; I played in the Little League. But mainly I was interested in sports where I could accomplish something myself without having to depend on others. There were friends around, but when you live in the country, your closest friends are three miles away."

Skiing was LeMond's major sport then, and from downhill he turned to freestyle skiing, attracted by its mix of showmanship and acrobatic skill. "I wanted something more challenging than going up a ski lift and whizzing back down." At thirteen he bought his first bicycle, earning the money by mowing lawns at a real-estate development near his home. His yearning for a ten-speed bicycle had nothing to do with sports, he remembers, but with his need for transportation, just to get around.

The next year, 1975, LeMond was still hoping to become a champion hot-dog skier, and he watched the sport avidly on television. Seeking to learn some secrets, he enrolled in a training camp near Vancouver, British Columbia, where he was told that bicycle riding was an ideal exercise in the off-season. "It was the first time that I thought about my bike as anything but a form of transportation," he said.

At about the same time, LeMond and his father watched their first bicycle road race as the Nevada state championships rolled past their home. The boy was impressed with the speed and action of the race, and especially with the physical fitness of the riders. When he returned from the freestyle skiing school, he began training on his bicycle in earnest. So did his father, who was eager to lose twenty pounds, and that fall the two of them began riding about twenty miles a day. Soon their program expanded to longer rides and climbs over mountain passes in the Washoe Valley. "Skiing became secondary," LeMond recalled, especially when the winter of 1975-76 produced little snow.

Driving across the mountains to northern California, the LeMonds went nearly every weekend to intermediate races— with competitors between thirteen and fifteen years old—for the boy and senior races for his father. "Most of the races in our district, northern California and Nevada, were in the Bay Area," Gordis recalled. "Greg would stay with us overnight so he could race Saturday and Sunday. Usually the whole family would come to the races—Bob, Bertha, and Greg's sisters Kathy and Karen. His family was supportive right from the start. Bob took up cycling at thirty-five, and at the age of thirty-eight or so he got fifth in the Coors Classic." Gordis whistled in admiration as he said this.

A question often asked about LeMond is where he got his strength and stamina. For Gordis, the answer is simple. "Purely genetic," he said. "He was born like this. I remember going riding with Greg and Bob up the Virginia City Grade— it's about seventy-five miles long—and when I got to Carson City, ten miles from the LeMond house, I bonked." Both verb and noun, "bonk" is how riders describe a sudden collapse. "I was weaving across the road," he remembered. "Very embarrassing. Bob didn't bonk, and of course Greg didn't either. It's something in the genes."

Throughout this period, LeMond has recalled, his father encouraged him and spent money willingly on new equipment and clothing. "I was lucky that my dad was so involved and loved the sport so much," he remembered, leaving unstated his father's devotion. As his interest grew, LeMond began to buy bicycling magazines and store away their tips on training and nutrition. He also studied their articles about European racing, and admired the photographs of stars laboring up mountain passes that resembled those near his home.

In short, LeMond was hooked. His fascination was reinforced by visits to the nearby workshop of Roland Della Santa, a master bicycle-frame builder who was also one of LeMond's sponsors and crafted his first custom bicycles. "Roland's place is like a bicycle museum, with all the old Italian bicycle magazines and posters," recalled Jeff Sanchez, another LeMond boyhood friend, "and that bug is catching."

LeMond caught it. "Once or twice a week I went to Roland's shop and hung out while he worked. He'd tell me stories about the great European stars, thousands of screaming fans and legendary races like the Tour de France and the Giro d'Italia."

Skiing was forgotten. "After I got into cycling, for the first five or six years I worked so hard at it that I never did anything else. I was so hooked that I didn't ski, hunt, or fish anymore. Not until I turned professional at nineteen and cycling became a real job did I go back to those sports as a release."

Working hard at bicycling and developing his talent, LeMond instantly became a winner. "He won his first four races in a row, and the first time he lost, I beat him," Gordis said proudly. "It was a 2.6-mile race outside Santa Cruz, California, four laps, and I don't think he was even warmed up because I beat him in a sprint."

LeMond didn't lose often, and victory became empty. "When I was fifteen years old I started racing in the intermediate class, and as soon as I won eight or nine races, I got tired of it. I didn't want to win all the time; I liked competition. So I asked permission to race with the juniors, and at first had a hard time with them, racing against seventeen- and eighteen-year-olds, but I got second place quite often. I was very competitive with that age group. I was only fifteen, going on sixteen, and I was beating guys seventeen or eighteen years old. When you're twenty-five, beating guys twenty-seven years old doesn't mean much, but when you're only a teenager there's a huge difference with older guys in all the important areas—stamina, training, strength, experience.

"The following year, at sixteen, I started winning all the junior races, chalking up thirty victories in one year. I'd win about half the time, lose about half the time—but losing meant getting second or third." The next year he began racing against seniors, riders eighteen and over, at the national level. Again he was quickly a winner.

"Although I had immediate success, I still wasn't sure how good I could be," LeMond remembered. "In 1977, I went to the U.S. junior world trials and won two out of three races. Though I won those two races, I couldn't be selected for the world championship team because I was too young, not yet old enough to be a junior. Then I won the national road race for juniors that year, and started beating even national-caliber seniors. I was still fifteen when I almost beat John Howard, then the top American senior rider, in one race."

Gordis remembered that race too. "It was the Tour of Fresno, a three-day race, and he finished one second behind

John Howard, the big American racer then. To imagine that a fifteen-year-old kid could almost beat John Howard was unthinkable."

The curve continued upward. "In 1978 I kept getting better," LeMond said. "In the spring of that year, I went to the junior worlds in Washington, D.C., where, I had written on the yellow pad, I wanted to get experience, and got a ninth in the road race. We also got a third in the team time trial," in which a team of four rides against the clock. "I was the anchor guy, the strongest rider on the team, so I didn't have any doubts about my ability in America, and once I got to winning at the senior level, I wanted to move on."

In the summer of 1978, LeMond went to Europe for the first time, traveling with Gordis and his mother and father. "I arranged that summer to go with Kent for two months to Switzerland, France, and Belgium and stay with his family. In Europe I started racing and winning, five or six quick races.

"But that wasn't even the best of it. I still remember getting off the plane in Switzerland. It was so beautiful! After thirty minutes there I said, 'God, Kent, I've always heard of culture shock but I don't feel any here!' Then about a week later I started feeling homesick. I missed my family, missed the American weather, missed everything except American food.

"That's when I first started developing my expensive tastes in nice restaurants," said LeMond sardonically. He fancies himself a gourmet and will strongly deny, despite the hamburger in his hand and the bowl of corn chips on the table, that he is a king of junk food.

In Europe, LeMond and Gordis were on territory they had dreamed about as fans. "At that time, cycling in America was like a secret society," Gordis said of their boyhood years. "We'd sit around and read cycling magazines, like the French *Miroir du Cyclisme*. I used to go to the French-American bookstore in San Francisco, where you could buy a three-month-old

Miroir. You know how kids find names like 'Bali' or 'Tahiti' exotic? We found all those unpronounceable Flemish names in *Miroir* exotic. We'd amuse ourselves by repeating the names to each other: Herman van der Slagmolen, Flèche Wallone, or whatever. Going to Europe for us was not just a trip abroad; it was attaining some sort of exalted state."

LeMond picked up the story. "I was riding in Switzerland against juniors, but they were European juniors," he recalled. "I was racing against the best. I won almost every road race I entered and started gaining confidence. I started thinking, 'Hey, maybe I *am* better than just the average junior.' In fact I already knew that I really was better than the average junior, but I'd always felt that Europe was where the competition was. No matter how many races I won in America, no matter what seniors I beat there, it was nothing compared to the Europeans.

"For a time-out, I flew back from Switzerland for the national championships in America—I was the defending champion and had to do it—and got second before flying back to Belgium to meet the Gordis family again. They were going there for vacation, primarily for me, because I wanted to race in Belgium after the races in Switzerland. In the three weeks I was in Belgium I won three races, but I found what really tough racing meant. The junior races were about sixty miles long, whereas in America the average junior race was twenty to thirty miles long—nothing! I was racing two or three times a week over cobblestones, into a strong wind. The racing was about twice as hard as the top-level amateur racing in America. Well, I'd said I was looking for competition."

The three races that he won built LeMond's confidence and furthered his racing education. He began to understand bicycling tactics, how to race against Europeans and how to race into the wind and along narrow roads. He was laying the foundation for his professional career.

"What an experience! I got through it all fine, learned a lot, and made up my mind that no matter what, Europe was where I wanted to be."

A few years later, the U.S. boycott of the 1980 Olympic Games in Moscow helped LeMond reach his goal. That spring, before President Carter announced his intention to boycott, LeMond trained with the Olympic bicycling team in Europe, riding in three races—the Circuit des Ardennes in Belgium, and the Circuit de la Sarthe and the Ruban Granatier Breton in France. Months shy of his nineteenth birthday, he was already known in the small world of bicycling because of his performance in 1979 at the junior world championships, where he had won three medals, including the gold for the road race. Although officials of European teams were impressed, they wrote off part of LeMond's domination because the championships had been held in Buenos Aires, where different time zones, food, and water often skewed results. How would he do against their best young amateurs when they were at home, riding on familiar roads and cheered by friends and relatives?

The answer came quickly: in the first race he won a stage, one day's part of a longer race, and finished third overall. "I also got some good press," LeMond recalled. Benefiting from being in better form once he became accustomed to Europe, he started fast in the next race, the Circuit de la Sarthe, coming in second in the time trial (an individual race against the clock), and winning the race overall. "It was the first time an American had ever won an international stage race," LeMond said proudly. "Also it was an open race, with amateurs like me and professionals too."

What would he do for an encore? "I had attracted some attention, and Cyrille Guimard, the manager of the Renault team, came and watched me one day," LeMond remembered.

It was nearly the wrong day. Racing in the Ruban Granatier in Brittany, LeMond had finished second in two stages and was in fourth or fifth place overall (he no longer remembers, though all the other details of that afternoon remain firmly in his mind). He was five minutes ahead of the pack, the main group of riders, when his troubles began. "I was chasing three Russians on a breakaway and I was ten seconds behind them and moving up fast when I punctured. The French mechanic who was supposed to be looking out for our team had been sleeping in his car, and he finally came up to me about ten kilometers after my accident; I'd ridden that far on a flat tire. By the time he got to me the field was about thirty seconds behind me and the breakaway was about four minutes ahead of me. There was no way I could win the race, thanks to that mechanic, and he was insisting that I get back on the bike and try to get third place. I was so mad I couldn't see straight."

Kathy LeMond continued the story. "He threw his bike at the team car," she explained.

"They cost me the race," LeMond responded in self-defense. Team cars are usually no more than a minute away. "Then the mechanic told me I had to continue, for the good name of the team."

"Then he threw his bike into the grass at the side of the road," Kathy went on. LeMond added: "So somebody said to Guimard, 'Do you want a racer like that?' and Guimard answered, 'Now I want him. He's got character.' "

When he first told this story to a reporter in 1982, LeMond looked pleased with the support that he said Guimard had offered. He was not a bit abashed by a reminder that in Guimard's version of the story the last line is "He's got character, but no more nonsense like that."

In any event, Guimard, who was known for his ability to spot and sign the best young riders for the Renault team, approached LeMond after the race and said, "We're really interested in you. I know you won the junior world championship last year and I've been following you since. I think you've got the potential to become a good professional. We want you to join our team. Will you meet with us in Paris in a week to discuss a contract?''

"What could I say?'' LeMond asked rhetorically in recalling the conversation.

LeMond went to Paris a week later to meet Guimard, as well as the Peugeot team, which was also interested in hiring him. These were professional employers, not the sponsors who had furthered his career as an amateur with stipends. He decided that Renault and Guimard were better suited to his needs, and promised to sign a contract after the Olympics. "There was already some talk that there would be no American team at the Olympics, and I said that if this happened, I'd return to France and discuss the deal again.

"Back home I went to the Olympic trials and ended up winning the road race and making the team. But there was very little hope that we were going to Moscow, and we knew it, so I wasn't heartbroken when the boycott was announced. Anyway, in cycling the Olympics are just a stepping-stone. For a cyclist, the Tour de France is where the best competition is. That's what cycling's all about.

"I felt I had the talent to be one of the best, and that's why I never hesitated about going to Europe. By now I felt that every step of my way I'd always been one of the best.

"Anyway, I don't think I've missed anything in life by turning professional at nineteen. Well, maybe a college education, but what I've learned in all my contract negotiations, learning French, seeing the world—that's at least a two-year education. I might not have a master's degree in business, but business-wise I'm pretty smart.

"The only thing I may have missed is having a solid base in an organized life. We have two households, we see friends for only two or three months of the year, and I'm always off traveling. But I know that this is a once-in-a-lifetime chance, and I would never have done anything differently. There are always career regrets; for example, I believe that if I were Dutch or French or Italian it would be much easier to get sponsors and to form a team around me. I'm not saying that this would be better for my cycling, but it would give me peace of mind because I'd know that everybody on the team was there for me.

"But as far as personal regrets go, I have none. How many guys can race their bikes, make a lot of money, and see the world?"

3

"Me and Kathy Against the World"

Nobody on the Renault team wanted to room with Greg LeMond in the early years because, ma foi, *the American did not understand that air was not good for you. At night he liked to keep the windows open. As good Frenchmen, the others had known since childhood about the evil effect of fresh air in a room, especially while one slept. But somebody had to share the room and finally Vincent Barteau volunteered. The American was such a good guy, so easy to get along with even if he barely spoke their language, so ready to laugh and enjoy himself, that maybe a little fresh air was worth the price. They became close friends and Barteau began visiting LeMond in the United States. When his career began to decline, Barteau knew he could always count on his friend Greg to find him a job on his new team. He was not LeMond's mascot—he bridled at the suggestion—but his friend, and as Barteau liked to say, Greg looked out for his friends.*

NEAR THE MIDDLE of his long comeback after being shot, Greg LeMond registered a small victory in the 1988 Tirreno–

Adriatico race across Italy. Even "small" is too big a word for finishing first in one of the handful of bonus sprints during a daily stage, but for LeMond it was his first victory in more than a year and he was determined to mark the occasion. Instead of buying champagne to celebrate when his team sat down for dinner that evening, he ordered ice cream. To most people ice cream is a dessert, but to LeMond it's a cause and a metaphor.

"I'm the type that, if they say 'Don't eat ice cream,' I'll probably eat a gallon of it," he said. "I probably never would have eaten any, but because they say 'Don't,' I'll go down and buy a gallon and eat it in front of them. Then I'll try even harder to do well the next day just to show them that it doesn't make a difference."

During his early years in Europe, LeMond remembers, he fought continually with the Renault team over his devotion to ice cream. "French riders have very fixed ideas about what's good for your racing," LeMond continued. "Ice cream is bad for you, but cheese is fine. Wine is okay, but pizza is bad. They think that whatever is good or bad is determined by whether it's in the tradition of cycling. Don't try to argue with them about fat content; what really matters is whether a certain food has been eaten by racers for generations."

For an American rider, Kent Gordis says, Europe can be a velvet trap. "We approached it with too much respect," he said of his and LeMond's first trip there. "A lot of Americans—though maybe not Greg—regard European racing with too much reverence."

Although the European concept of diet did not make sense to LeMond, he has been known to flip-flop on the question. "When Greg and I trained and raced, my mom would make us fruit salad and we would eat three or four huge salad bowls of it," Gordis remembers. "In American racing, at that time, the theory was that you had to eat organic food, and the first few months I knew Greg he was following this ethic. Not just organic food but organic grape gruel, a very strict, powerful diet.

"Well, we went to a race in central California called the Pacific Something or Other Criterium and I raced terribly. Greg, as an intermediate, was racing with the juniors, and I figured, "If Greg is going to race with the juniors, so am I. But of course I didn't keep up the way he did. I got lapped after five or six laps. Afterward I was so depressed that I wanted to get a quart of ice cream and pig out." The event must have been traumatic; years later Gordis remembers the name of the ice cream store. "Greg was shocked. He wouldn't talk to me. But of course the next time I went to his house, there he was eating a bucket of ice cream. He would eat two or three bowls of ice cream, a hot dog, and a hamburger almost to shock you. It was as if he were saying, 'Here I can sit down, have two bowls of ice cream and still hammer you in a race.' "

Whether to shock or as a matter of principle, LeMond has continued to enjoy what European riders regard as an offbeat diet. "He could unearth a Mexican restaurant in the depths of the Auvergne," sniffed the French sports newspaper *L'Equipe* in an otherwise admiring article after LeMond's second Tour de France victory. (In fact, LeMond has already made reservations at a Mexican restaurant, The Sombrero, in Poitiers, deep in the countryside near the start of the 1990 Tour.) Like everybody else in professional bicycling, the writer for *L'Equipe* knew that LeMond has startled his teammates in the Tour by unexpectedly cooking Tex-Mex meals for them with ingredients supplied by his wife from exotic-food stores in Belgium. When one of his earlier teams, La Vie Claire, sent a group of riders including LeMond and Bernard Hinault to the Coors Classic in 1986, LeMond tried vainly to interest his teammates in American cuisine.

"The French are great cooks and I really like their cuisine, but that's all they eat," LeMond complained. "They won't even *try* other foods. In America, Hinault was an exception; the other riders weren't interested."

Despite his addiction to refried beans and tortilla chips, LeMond proudly considers himself a gourmet, especially liking the way Belgians cook French food. He is also knowledgeable about wine. Driving once to a minor race in Belgium, he pointed out to Steve Bauer, a Canadian friend and at that time teammate, various restaurants hidden down side roads while listening with grave attention to Bauer's story about a restaurant he had dined in recently. "We had foie gras," Bauer said, "and there was a sweet wine with it . . ."

"Sauternes," LeMond instructed.

"And then a red, Roth something . . ."

"Rothschild," LeMond prompted. "Mouton Rothschild."

These eclectic tastes of LeMond's make for trouble at the training table; Renault has not been the only employer to complain about his eating habits. "His whole career he could eat hamburgers, not take care about what he drank and when to rest," said an official of the PDM team after LeMond left it. "He's so good that he can live like ordinary people," the man continued in grudging admiration. "When he was with us, he was too fat and he was still eating his hamburgers and pizzas, drinking his beers."

PDM is a Dutch team and somewhat Calvinist in outlook. Renault, however, was French, and therefore the dispute, as in so many arguments with the French about food, was really about the liver. "They're obsessed with their livers," LeMond says, echoing generations of Americans who have been mystified by the Gallic fascination with that organ. "I remember Hinault saying in the Tour of Italy once, 'Someone gave me an ice cream, and about five kilometers down the road I had a liver attack, a *crise de foie*.' 'For sure it was that ice cream,' I said. He didn't realize I was being sarcastic."

LeMond recalls nightly arguments with the Renault masseurs about ice cream. "Chocolate was bad for your liver, ice cream was bad for your liver, pastries were bad for your liver. They got it all mixed up. The fat might be bad because excess fat isn't good for your arteries, but it's not bad for your *liver*; what's bad for your liver is alcohol. But they said, 'No, wine is good for your blood and has nothing to do with your liver.'

"For years I would skip the cheese and yogurt that the Renault riders had as a last course. I like both of them but they're high in fat. If I was going to eat something like that, I'd rather have a bowl of ice cream. But I'd have to eat it on the sly because the other riders were so sure it was bad for your liver.

"Through it all, I insisted on eating that ice cream. I've never been one to try to be like a Frenchman or an Italian. I want to stay the way I am. I enjoy being the person I am. My wife, Kathy, feels the same way, and it was our determination to stay American that helped us get through some bad times emotionally when we first went to Europe. For a while it seemed to be me and Kathy against the world."

"Me and Kathy against the world," or, as the grammatically careful LeMond usually puts it, "Kathy and I against the world," became a familiar refrain after the hunting accident as well. It was easy to forget that the young couple, teenage sweethearts, had been married nearly a decade when LeMond won the Tour de France for the second time. They had met in 1978, at the national bicycling championships in Milwaukee, where LeMond was palling around with another amateur rider, Greg Demgen, from La Crosse, Wisconsin, also the hometown of Kathy Morris. She came to nearby Milwaukee to visit Demgen, "who had gone to grade school with her and had a big crush on her," LeMond remembered. "As I found out later, Kathy liked him, but not as a boyfriend. She and her sister came down and we all went out that night. My date was Kathy's sister, Lisa."

The next time LeMond saw Kathy Morris was a year later when he nearly won the Coors Classic, then called the Red Zinger, just after his eighteenth birthday. She and a friend visited for a week, LeMond says, adding, "Demgen and I went out with them almost every night to dinner and the movies. This was during the race. That was the kind of life I lived in American cycling, which was why it was so hard to live like a monk in Europe. It was supposedly the hardest American race, but still we would race, get a massage, eat dinner and go to a movie. Imagine having the energy, or even the desire, to go to a movie after a stage of the Tour de France! Still, during the Red Zinger we'd go to bed by eleven o'clock because we weren't all that foolish."

Jeff Sanchez, who knew LeMond as a youth in Nevada, would laugh at that. "He was a wild kid," Sanchez remembers affectionately. "He wouldn't want to train a lot; he'd get into trouble and drink beer. Or he and a friend would skip school, go skiing, and stay out late." He smiled at the memory. "His father would be after him all the time to train."

Asked about this, LeMond breaks into a huge smile. "Wild? Me? No," he says, drawing the "No" out. "Never."

The racer Ron Kiefel shakes his head in disagreement. He was a teammate of LeMond's in the 1978 team time trial at the junior world championships in Washington, and has raced with and against him for a decade. "He definitely had some wild streaks in the late seventies," Kiefel said, although his definition of a wild streak may be straight out of *Leave It to Beaver*. "We'd go out and drink or go dancing and raise some hell. He's always had so much energy. But he could do that and come back and win the race the next day while the rest of us would suffer." Kiefel's face twisted at the recollection of his own pain. "He was wild, but he didn't do anything malicious or break anything." Discretion kept him from saying more.

When LeMond went to La Crosse for the 1979 national championships, he and Kathy began going out together.

"I started falling for her and I could tell she liked me. We had a lot of good times. From then on it was a long-distance love affair. I'd saved up about seven thousand dollars from racing; I'd bought a BMW and had about three thousand dollars in the bank, trying to build up some assets. But I ended up spending a hundred and fifty to two hundred dollars a month on phone bills to Kathy—a lot of money. I was scheming every possible way to see her. I flew out at the end of August to a race in Minneapolis, came down to La Crosse and met her parents and saw her for a couple of weeks there. Then I had to go to Colorado to prepare for the junior world championships, and we kept writing and phoning every day.

"From Buenos Aires, where the 1979 junior worlds were held, we couldn't talk much, but I told her that if I won, I'd call her immediately after the road race. About twenty minutes after my victory, I went to the press box to call her and she answered, really excited. I was cool and said, 'Hi, Kathy, how are you doing?' And she said, 'Fine, but how did *you* do?' And I couldn't stay cool. 'I won!' I burst out."

When he returned from Argentina, LeMond went to Minneapolis and spent a week with Kathy before he had to go home and finish high school. Then she came out to visit him in Nevada. That December LeMond returned to Minneapolis, where Kathy was attending Gustavus Adolphus College, and the two of them went to a jewelry store and bought a two-thousand-dollar engagement ring. "That was the end of my savings," LeMond joked.

Both still teenagers, Greg and Kathy were married late in 1980, even though originally they had planned to remain engaged for several years until Kathy finished college. What changed their minds was LeMond's decision to sign his first professional contract and move to Europe. They decided to go together. "Her mom and dad were shocked when we told them that we wanted to get married; they were really upset that she wanted to marry a bike rider. They had no idea what cycling was. I was awfully young, and they said, 'How is he going to support you? What if he doesn't win?' It wasn't a big hassle, but I had to convince her parents that we were meant to be married. I tried to convince them that I was a responsible person, that my physical age might be nineteen but that I was really a couple of years older than that mentally. And I was. At that point I'd been to Europe several times, and it was as if I had a paying job: I made about thirty thousand dollars that year from prizes and sponsors."

LeMond carried the day, and the couple set off for France, where he had a stint as an amateur racer before turning professional. "Kathy and I were engaged and I wanted her with me because we needed to get to know each other," LeMond says. "It was a great trip for getting to know each other—three or four weeks together.

"We started out very young, and we learned that there are deceptions and disappointments in life. When I signed my professional contract, that's when we started getting a bad taste of France. People think that when I first went to Europe I was hard, but I've been burned in business with empty promises so many times that now we always have a lawyer and get everything in writing. A lot of people will make promises, say, 'Yes, yes, yes,' but when it comes to putting it in writing and living up to the promises, it gets difficult."

The LeMonds went to Paris, where he planned to race for three months for U.S. Créteil, a major amateur bicycle club just outside the city. Their first disappointment came when LeMond learned that Créteil planned to let him race only once a week, which he could have done in the United States. He wanted three races a week, and difficult ones.

The second disappointment came from Lejeune, the bicycle manufacturer that sponsored the club, which had promised the couple a car and a furnished apartment but instead delivered no car and an unfurnished apartment inhabited by another couple. For three weeks LeMond barely raced, and he and Kathy spent nights in hotels that he described as "dives near the train stations, which cost ten dollars a night." Their rooms were full of bicycles and suitcases.

Unhappy and rapidly running out of money, the couple was tempted by an invitation from the U.S. Olympic Committee to visit the White House as compensation for the 1980 Olympic boycott. LeMond was not unhappy that he had missed the Olympics and did not feel that he needed compensation, but the offer was a face-saving way out of Europe. The weekend he signed his professional contract with Renault, he and Kathy decided there was no reason to stay in Paris. "My God, we were so happy to get home."

LeMond and Kathy were married on December 21, 1980. "I have to admit I did too much celebrating in La Crosse and gained about fifteen pounds," LeMond said with a laugh. "In a word, I was fat. I was so much smaller musclewise at that time than I am now, and my best weight then was a hundred and forty-three pounds; so I must have weighed a hundred and fifty-eight. Now I weigh a hundred fifty to a hundred and fifty-five pounds but have much more muscle; I've really filled out. After we got married we went out to San Diego and I trained for ten days just to get in decent shape."

Before he signed the Renault contract with Guimard, LeMond told him how disappointed he had been with the broken promises of U.S. Créteil. "But they're an amateur team," said another Renault official. "Us, we're professionals.

I could find you a furnished house or apartment like that," and he snapped his fingers.

LeMond happily signed with Renault a contract that called for a furnished house and a car. But when the couple arrived in France in January of 1981, Greg's Renault car proved to be a lemon, complete with a warped windshield that prevented the driver from seeing the road clearly. Nevertheless they drove to Nantes, a city in Brittany near Guimard's hometown. Guimard wanted the couple, who spoke no French, to live nearby so that he could watch over them. There they discovered that the promised house was not yet ready and that Renault had booked them into a hotel in the town where Guimard lived. LeMond remembers the hotel as small, with "pretty good food, except that Kathy got food poisoning." For two weeks they lived there in a small room, with toilets and showers down the hall. "It rained every day. I trained a hundred kilometers a day four or five times a week and it rained, rained, rained. I simply couldn't get in shape. Plus we had no car because something else was wrong with it besides the windshield and they took it away." Finally, early in February, Guimard found the couple a three bedroom house just before LeMond left for his first race, the Etoile de Bessèges, which traditionally opens the cycling season in France.

LeMond's introduction to his new way of life came late one afternoon when he boarded the team bus, leaving home for the race and four or five weeks of competition. "After three hours of driving we had to stop for dinner," he recalled. "This was France, after all. After a two-hour dinner we got back on the bus, drove another hour, and stopped at a hotel to sleep. In the morning, we got back in the bus, drove about three hours, and stopped for lunch. I was getting a taste of what it's like to live in Europe, and what I thought was, 'Let's just get there! *Then* we'll have lunch!' Instead we drove, stopped for dinner again, and finally, after starting at four P.M. the day before, we reached Bessèges about seven P.M. the next night, with a race the next day. When we finally got there I was exhausted; it was like flying from the U.S. to Europe. It had taken twenty-seven hours to travel what would take seven hours nonstop."

Since he spoke no French, LeMond was the odd man out at team meals. Renault tried to help him by hiring another American rider, Jonathan (Jock) Boyer, who had lived in Europe for years and spoke fluent French, but the two did not hit it off. "That whole February I went through about fifteen espionage novels, mostly by Robert Ludlum; that's how bored I was," LeMond remembers. "I'd come to dinner and Jock would say, 'Greg, it's rude of you to read at the table.' And I'd say, 'But I don't speak French. I've been sitting here every day, listening to everybody laugh and chat, and I don't understand a thing they say. I'm bored; this is my only form of escape.' I read and read."

Life was no better for Kathy. When money ran low, Renault suggested that she move into the rented house, which had no furniture, heat, or hot water. "We hadn't been paid my salary yet," LeMond said. "We spent all our wedding money waiting for a check. It was a disaster. I could have said, 'Forget it, I don't want to race here ever again.' Now that I have money, we know how to live in France and it's wonderful. But we really had a terrible introduction. Renault did not do its best. It tried to act like an organized, professional team, but it really wasn't. Guimard's wife was supposed to be looking out for us after Cyrille went off to the races, but she didn't care.

"My mom came over for two weeks and she and Kathy lived without hot water. They bought hot plates to cook on because there was no stove. All they had was a sink. They were freezing and starving to death. Kathy started drinking coffee for the first time in her life, just to stay warm. She and my mom had foldout cots surrounded by mousetraps; that's how rough it was.

"We didn't get the furniture until April twentieth. Two and a half months! Mrs. Guimard is still angry at Kathy because she called her every day to ask what was happening and Mrs. Guimard would say, 'The furniture is on the way from Strasbourg.' Kathy didn't know where that was; she didn't realize that it was in eastern France, only a few hundred miles away. Mrs. Guimard told her not to leave the house; if the furniture showed up, she had to be there to sign for it, so Kathy and my mom never left the house together.

"Kathy would go over to Mrs. Guimard's house, screaming and crying, saying, 'We're freezing cold, there's no heat, we can't take a bath and we can't afford to go to a hotel,' and Mrs. Guimard would say, 'The furniture's coming, I'm doing everything I can,' and shoo her out the door. When we moved to Belgium, people would have given us furniture, insisted that we borrow from them."

That summer of 1981 LeMond returned to the United States to ride and win the Coors Classic. He became sick but came back to France to race criteriums—short exhibition races through a town or city streets—for three or four hundred dollars. "It was freezing cold and I was burning up inside. I didn't want to do them, but I stuck it out. I wanted to make it in cycling. I trained hard; I did nine-hour rides around Nantes once or twice a week to get rid of my fat. I was dedicated, all right.

"Kathy and I came from nice homes, with nice families and lots of friends. In Europe we had no friends, no house, no furniture, no money—*nothing*. We didn't speak French and there were no American movies; everything was dubbed into French. In those days there wasn't even a McDonald's or a Burger King, as there are now, where you could go in Nantes to get a cheeseburger just to remind you of home. Every time we could we'd escape to Belgium and I'd do a training ride and race a couple of times. We'd stay at a hotel and watch a movie in English. We'd go into a store and see . . . cheddar cheese! Cap'n Crunch! Stuff we just freaked out about."

The next year LeMond broke his collarbone in a fall, and with a month off from racing they went to Belgium again. "We stayed in a beautiful room in a hotel that had BBC television. We'd go into town and have a waffle, then see a movie in English. Finally we said, 'Why are we living in Nantes? Let's move!' That September, after two years in Nantes, we found a house in Kortrijk and moved in the next winter. It's been heaven.

"When people heard that we were moving to Belgium, I felt as if I were telling the French public that I didn't like their country. But as I said to the press, 'Pretend a Frenchman is coming to America and at first his company puts him in Iowa. But it turns out he can live anywhere. Wouldn't he move to Quebec or Montreal, where he can speak French?' I didn't mention that the main reason we were in Nantes was that Cyrille Guimard wanted me nearby, but the whole two years I was there I saw him only once socially.

"Now when North American riders come over here they talk about living in the south of France. I say to them, 'Why not try Belgium?' At first sight it's not the most beautiful country, but when you get past the weather and into a town like Kortrijk, Bruges, or Ghent, it's very good living. The advantage of living in Europe and being able to talk English keeps me sane."

4

Triumphs and Troubles

A few months short of his thirty-ninth birthday, Joop Zoetemelk had just won the 1985 world championship road race, and everybody agreed that it made a wonderful ending for his long career. Big victories didn't often come his way: six times he finished second in the Tour de France, a race he won only once, in 1980. This was the Dutchman's fifteenth world championship race in his fifteen years as a professional and never before had he finished higher than fourth. Among the first to congratulate him was Greg LeMond, who had finished second, three seconds behind but winning the gang sprint for the silver medal. "Wonderful race, Joop," LeMond cried out. He was sincere, LeMond said later. If somebody else had to win, it should be Zoetemelk. Had LeMond held back in any way to let the old man have his final moment of glory? LeMond was shocked by the question. That was not what the sport was all about, he said; it was all about winning.

FAR FROM HOME and twenty years old, LeMond began his apprenticeship in the trade and world he had chosen. It was not an easy life. Professional bicycling is unlike, say, baseball, with its vast gap between luxury hotels and jet travel in the major leagues, and seedy locker rooms and buses in the minors. In professional bicycling, life at the top is not much better than life at the bottom.

Even in the Tour de France, riders are rarely housed in better than a modest hotel. Often a team will find itself lodged in a youth hostel or a dormitory left vacant for the summer, its rows of beds covered with mattresses folded in half. In their first year as professionals, young riders are astounded to see veterans ranked among the best in the world awaiting their turn at a communal sink to rinse out their jersey for the next day's stage. Having been installed in the sort of hotel that does not make the Guide Michelin but is cheap for the organizers, riders complain of traffic noise under their windows at night. Often the bathroom is down the hall, and sometimes an extra bed has been squeezed into a room just large enough for two. In the first Tour de Trump through the northeast United States in 1989, European riders were surprised and delighted by their accommodations—color television, private bathrooms, a maximum of two men to a room—in the sort of chain hotels that most American travelers regard as adequate though hardly luxurious.

LeMond learned quickly to accept the rigors of his new life from the 100-kilometer-long criteriums, where the local hero or big-name rider was usually allowed to win, to the 250-kilometer, demanding classics, where the real glory in day-long races was to be found and competition was genuine, to the ultimate tests, the three-week Tours of Spain, Italy, and, of course, France. "I've gutted it out," he says proudly. Few other American riders on European teams could say the same; nearly all of them disappear from the circuit after a season or two. "There's hardly been anybody else," LeMond confirms. "Jock Boyer is the only one I can think of. Despite our earlier differences, I can truthfully say he had a pretty good career. Boyer deserves respect; at the age of thirty-two in 1987, he was still able to finish the Tour for the 7-Eleven team, and in 1983 he placed as high as twelfth. He won the Race Across America too, which can be pretty grueling."

When LeMond broke in with Renault in 1981, he and Boyer were the only two Americans riding for major European teams. Although Renault hired Boyer as a companion and guide for the young LeMond, six years his junior, they could not get along. Now retired from racing but still based in Europe for his California bicycle-importing company, Boyer is a likeable, sometimes sardonic man who did not really begin to relax until he felt he had gained professional respect. But that arrived later in his career, not by 1981.

"When we came together," LeMond remembered, "I was nineteen. When I showed up in Paris that January, Boyer had been racing for four or five years in Europe, dedicating himself to being a professional. So here's this young American—a kid, really—who comes to Europe highly touted. I got whirlwind press and it had a psychological effect on Jock. I can't blame him. It happens now to me, too. I hear other American riders—not Andy Hampsten, guys nowhere near his class—say, 'I'm going over there to win the mountain jersey in the Tour.' They feel free to say that because they were decent riders in the Coors Classic. Big deal! They have absolutely no idea what it takes.

"I think Boyer felt that way too when I came over with some very positive attitudes and said, 'Maybe I can win a race or two this year.' He hadn't really won much in his whole career and here I was, nineteen years old, confident that I could win a race or two right off the bat. He knew how hard it was and I didn't. Immediately we started rubbing each other wrong. That whole year he acted jealous of me; I got to not like him and we had bitter fights.

"Now we both see how childish it was that we were fighting over petty jealousies. We'll probably never be close friends, but I think we regard each other with a little more respect than we had then. Boy, was it tough at the start. The worst moment was when people accused me of costing Boyer the world road-race championship in 1982 in Goodwood, England."

This was not the first, and certainly not the last, controversy LeMond has been involved in during the world championships. Racing affects his personality, LeMond admits: "When I race, my mind completely changes. I get much more aggressive." By this LeMond does not mean he elbows other riders aside or screams at them in an attempt at intimidation, as some other great cyclists have done. "Aggressive" is his way of saying he becomes single-minded and decisive about his chances of winning. Affable and relaxed off his bicycle, he is concentrated and tough on it, especially in a major race. And he gives high priority to the annual world championship professional road race, ranking it below only the Tour de France in prestige.

The title of world champion is highly regarded among professional riders, who acknowledge that a one-day race rarely proves much, but then point out that a long list of stars have won it. While he voices the usual criticism, LeMond emphasizes the championship race's importance and almost always rides well in it.

The race is held in a different country each year, near the end of August, as part of the two-week-long world championships for amateur and professional riders on roads and tracks. As an American, LeMond has been handicapped by rarely having a strong team working for him, since the road-race championship is organized by nations rather than professional teams. (Until a few years ago, the United States could not field a full twelve-man squad.) "I've never had a real team there," LeMond says.

The troubled feelings between LeMond and Boyer came to a peak at the 1981 world championship, LeMond's first as a professional, which was held in Prague. At that time the world championship road race counted as the American national championship as well. "In those days—and it isn't really so long ago, which shows how far cycling has come in America in less than a decade—it wasn't worth anybody's bother to have a professional championship since most American riders were amateurs," LeMond recalls. "So after the 1980 world championship, Jock had himself declared national and professional American champion because he was the best-placed American. The whole next year he got to race in a star-spangled jersey, just like the American flag, as national champion."

Whether this bothered LeMond, he does not say. He insists that he objected only to the principle involved. "I had made it clear before the race in Prague that I was not going to race the world championship as the national championship and have myself competing against other Americans instead of us all working together. I said absolutely not." Every other country had its national championship in June, on the Sunday just before the start of the Tour de France. Then those countries sent a team to the world championship to work together and try to help a rider from their country win. Of course there was often still some team interaction; a Dutch rider might be wearing his country's orange jersey, but if somebody from his sponsored team—an Italian, say—had a good chance of winning, the Dutch rider would probably help him if no other Dutchman had a chance of winning. "It's very difficult to ride on a sponsored team all year long and then put that aside for one day a year to ride on national teams. But the whole point was that the guys on, say, the Dutch team didn't enter the race riding against each other to see who would become the national champion. That's the spirit I wanted."

In Prague the other members of the American team were willing to vote on whether they would race the worlds as a national championship. "Not me," LeMond said. "I didn't want to vote. My position was firm." He told the U.S. officials leading the team, "You can start the race without me if we're racing the national championship. All you're looking at is a race within a race. That's not farsighted enough," he remembers saying. "We should be racing with each other and against the Europeans, not against ourselves."

When the issue was put to a vote among the six riders on the American team, two went with Boyer and two with LeMond. According to LeMond's version, an American official then said, "Since it's a tie, I'll vote, and I vote that we make it the national championship."

" 'Fine,' I said, 'but you race without me,' and I walked out. The guy came running after me, yelling, 'You can't do that, you said we could vote it.'

"And I said, 'You voted and you won, but I'm not racing. If you want me to race, I'm racing the world championship for the world championship.' Was I being unfair or acting like a spoiled kid? Was I breaking my word? I don't think so, not at all. Let the majority rule, but don't let them force everybody else to do what they want. I was convinced that my position was best for the American riders, that I was putting the team ahead of my own personal ambitions. If other people wanted to put themselves ahead of the team and if the team voted to let them, fine—but don't count on me to go along.

"It's a fine line we're talking about here, between being a spoiled kid and respecting your own integrity, but I'm still convinced that I had my priorities right. I wasn't saying that nobody else should race—just me. The right to decide whether I'll race belongs to me, not to the team.

"They gave in when they saw that otherwise I wouldn't start. None of us did particularly well in that world championship," he recalls, and the fighting was still vivid at the 1982 championship in Goodwood, England.

"Do I have any regrets about Boyer and Goodwood? Absolutely not."

Boyer had left Renault by then, joining the Sem team. Though still with Renault, LeMond had been considered too young to ride in that year's Tour, and spent the summer relaxing and riding in criteriums before beginning training for the world championship. "I trained really hard for two weeks before the world's," he says. "But the week before the race I got sick, really sick—from bad water, I think—so five or six days before the race, I almost decided to skip it and go to the Alps to train for the Tour de l'Avenir. But my wife's parents were coming to England all the way from Wisconsin and they had nonrefundable tickets, and my folks were coming too, so I felt obligated to be there."

Just before the race, the Americans had a team meeting and decided that each man was riding for himself. "Right back to where we were in Prague, but this time I wasn't fighting them anymore," LeMond said. "If that's what the team wanted, fine. No more fights, no more screaming at each other. We agreed that Greg LeMond was racing for Greg LeMond, and that Jock Boyer was racing for Jock Boyer.

"At the start I was so sick that I didn't even know if I wanted to race. But when I got into it, I started feeling pretty good. With three or four laps to go, I had made several attacks to get away, and guess who chased me down? Jock Boyer! When it came down to the last lap, there was a long uphill and Boyer attacked. I just sat there as he built a pretty good lead. With about five hundred or six hundred yards to go, I attacked and caught Boyer just like that, absolutely nothing to

45
.

it, which showed how strong I was and also how much he was weakening.

"At the same time, Giuseppe Saronni of the Italian team was on me, and I ended up getting second. I wasn't going for second; I was going for the victory. But I also wasn't trying to ruin it for Boyer. If I were just chasing Boyer down, I'd have caught him, sat on him, and gotten tenth place. He faded back into the field and got ninth or tenth place.

"That was one of the most exciting events in my career. Here I was, the highest-placed American ever! But Boyer cried afterward and complained that he'd have won if I hadn't moved on him. No way! First, it was clear that he'd raced for himself and that I was racing for myself. Second, even if I'd sat there and blocked for him, it was clear—and Boyer has to face this—that he has never been a sprinter or a finisher. When you take Saronni, Kelly, or even myself, there's no comparison between our finishing abilities and Boyer's. We all flew by him.

"Immediately after the race, I was hammered by the press and everyone else: how could you do that to your country? Nobody knew what our relationship was and how the U.S. team was working at the time. I was wearing a U.S. jersey, sure, but there really wasn't an American team and I definitely wasn't part of it. I paid for my own trip to England—my hotel bills, everything. There was no support from the U.S. federation. So I've never had any regrets because I felt I had a much better chance to win the world's than Boyer. It just happened that Saronni won."

LeMond's silver medal was the first of any color for an American in a professional-bicycling world championship. While he did receive some criticism for his tactics, the sport is much more interested in results than in might-have-beens; his second place stamped him as a young rider to watch. Two weeks later he won the Tour de l'Avenir (the Tour of the Future) by more than ten minutes, the largest margin in the history of this race for young professionals and for the world's best amateurs. "His victory doesn't surprise me," said Bernard Hinault, the leader of the Renault team and at that time the winner of four Tours de France. "He's a super racer. I consider him my potential successor."

Strong words indeed. As the 1982 season ended and LeMond returned home to the United States for rest and orthodontia to correct his underbite and remove the braces he still wore, he seemed on his way to the top. But the early part of 1983 was marked by health problems, which began when LeMond raced the Vuelta d'España, the Tour of Spain, with a bad cold. "I never recovered after that and wanted to quit cycling for a month or two to get my health back," he says. "I had a virus and was exhausted for three or four weeks." Instead of stopping, he reduced his training schedule for his next big race, the mountainous Dauphiné Libéré in France. "The weekend before the Dauphiné began, I raced two kermesses—just training rides, really—and the night after the second one, I came home so weak and depressed that I had five bottles of beer, sat on my couch at home, and fell asleep. The next day I raced and felt pretty good."

LeMond finished a strong fifth in the prologue of the Dauphiné, won the next day's stage, and recorded three stage victories before finishing second overall to Pascal Simon, a French rider. A few weeks later Simon was disqualified for doping and LeMond was moved up to first place. "When you win a race that way, it's a victory clear and simple because the guy who beat you probably wouldn't have been able to do it if he hadn't been taking illegal substances."

After a strong fourth place in the Tour of Switzerland, LeMond was again kept out of the Tour de France because of his age. He returned to America for three weeks while the Tour took place, trained hard, came back to Europe and rode about fifteen criteriums.

"I'd do a hundred kilometers' training in the morning, then a hundred-kilometer criterium at night. I ended up really fit. The week before the world championship in Switzerland, I knew that I was going to do something. I've never felt stronger. I was just floating. When you're training that well, nothing is hard.

"The night before the worlds I was so nervous, though, that I could barely sleep. I couldn't get anything out of my mind. At breakfast at the German hotel we were staying in, I ordered a pot of muesli, two hard-boiled eggs, bread, and orange juice from room service. I ended up eating nothing but five bites of muesli and an apple. My stomach was in a knot. I went over to Cyrille Guimard and said, 'I'm so nervous that I only slept four or five hours last night, and I'm so exhausted this morning that I don't know how I'm going to do.' And Guimard answered, 'Greg, you're going to do really well today. Before their best days, all great champions have a sleepless night because they know they can win.'

"That's the kind of thing Guimard was so good at. He said, 'Don't worry about being nervous. You're going to win.' Maybe he didn't actually say I was going to win; maybe he actually said, 'You're going to have a big day when you're nervous because you know you're going to do well.' Whatever, it made me feel good. That was Guimard's strength—one of them at least.

"It was a hard race, very hard, but I felt so good that nothing felt tough, not even dropping the only rider remaining with me at the front, Faustino Ruperez, a Spaniard, on the last hill. Everything went just the way I wanted, and I breezed across the finish as world champion.

"World champion: that's the greatest feeling. Even in winning the Tour de France, when you've got the yellow jersey you're so worried about keeping it that it almost takes away the glory of winning. In the world championship, when you cross the line first, you've won it. Then it sinks in.

"Of course the truth is that I'd ten times rather win the Tour de France than the world championship, but somehow for pure happiness that world championship was untouchable. I was twenty-two years old, and it was as if I'd finally made my mark in cycling.

"My only disappointment was that the victory was totally ignored by the American press and public. Back home hardly anybody heard of it. Maybe it got a little paragraph in some papers, maybe not. In Europe, the world champion is on page one of his country's papers and even on page one of other countries' as well. But at that time nobody in the U.S. cared that an American had become world champion.

"Athletes feed on recognition," LeMond went on. "But so does everybody else, whether they're lawyers, carpenters, or teachers. It's not just money that makes motivated people do their jobs well; it's also the feeling that people know and respect their performance."

LeMond came close to winning the world championship again in 1985, finishing second. As well as strong performances, controversies continued to follow him in that race.

In 1984, when the world championship was staged in Barcelona, he and Moreno Argentin, an Italian rider, became involved in a dispute over whether Argentin had demanded money to help LeMond, an illegal act in the sport. "He admitted later that he had something against me from the '83 worlds, when I won," LeMond says. "I had dropped him and he'd been taking a lot of bad press at home in Italy because he hadn't been able to stay with me, so the next year in Barcelona he sat right on my wheel the whole race," riding in LeMond's slipstream, or drafting. "I mean that: all race long! Any move I made, he was right there on my wheel, never helping out by letting me draft off his wheel to save some energy. I ended up watching twenty guys jump away with no effort at all, just riding away from me because they were working together and I had nobody except Argentin, sitting behind me. I was so frustrated. 'What's wrong?' I asked him. 'Why are you doing this? What have you got against me?'

"He said something like, 'We're friends, but give me some money, ten thousand dollars, and I'll work for you.' To be truthful, I knew at the time that it was sarcasm, said only to get me even angrier. But I was *so* angry that I decided not to take it. When the race ended, I told the press, 'He wanted money; he told me so.' I wish now I'd never done it because the controversy hurt Argentin tremendously, but it also taught him not to fool around with me. He gave away the world championship. He could have won that year as easily as I could have if we'd worked together. If he races against me and I race against him, we're watching only each other in a race that twenty people can win. But if he races against everybody and lets me do the same, then we're both strong contenders.

"Why did I let him get to me? Because I knew that if I did all the work, that if he just rode my wheel and saved his strength, he'd beat me at the end. It meant that if I raced my race, he'd win. It was very upsetting to me the way he acted and I certainly upset him when I told about his demanding money, but at the time I felt he deserved it. Italian journalists asked, 'Greg, why didn't you win?' I said, 'Argentin sat on my wheel and then wanted ten thousand dollars to race.' Boy, did that raise a storm in Italy for him.

"The next year in the world championship, Argentin was involved with me again but he raced correctly. The 1985 race was tactically different, and even though he didn't race against me and I didn't race against him, at the end we were second— me—and third—him—to Joop Zoetemelk, the Dutch rider.''

After two second places and a victory in the previous four world championships, great things were expected of LeMond in the 1986 race. The script seemed to have been crafted in Hollywood: a month after his first victory in the Tour de France, he rides for the title in Colorado when the United States is host to the world championships for the first time since 1912. With the Rockies for a backdrop, he rolls first across the finish line as the fans go wild.

Unfortunately, the script was not followed. On a raw, foggy day on the circuit around the grounds of the U.S. Air Force Academy, LeMond could do no better than seventh place as—speaking of revenge- -Argentin won.

"I was really sick before that race," LeMond explained. "I raced a little bit too much that year. Before then I was smarter, racing a certain amount, taking a break, then racing again. But in 1986 I had a hundred and thirty races- a hundred and thirty days of racing—by September first. All of them were big-time races; all of them were raced to win. None of them were criteriums. I did the Tour of Italy, the Tour of Switzerland, the Tour de France, the Coors Classic, and in all of them I was trying to win. I just got burned out and I paid the price in the world championships."

Shortly before the championships in Colorado Springs, LeMond caught the flu while riding in the Coors Classic. "I was wasted. When I went home and saw a doctor, the worst was over and I'd passed the fever, but my body was exhausted. When I got home and tried to train for the championships, I couldn't ride more than two hours a day for the whole week before the race. Finally, about three days before the worlds I did a five-hour ride and found I was going a little bit better. If the worlds had been only one week later, I'd have been in much better condition. There really was no time to recuperate after the Coors.

"I held a news conference in Colorado Springs and tried to

be honest with the press. I said that I'd been sick, and that it would be very difficult for me to win the race. When the day came, I stuck it out even though it was cold and rainy, just what I didn't need. But I'd never quit a world championship that I started, and I certainly wasn't going to set a precedent in my own country before my own fans.

"Well, I got a seventh place, which would be anticlimactic for a lot of riders, but for me, coming three days after I didn't think I'd even start, it was a good result. Few people know how badly I wanted to win that championship. I'd said publicly that it was going to be my race on my turf, back in the United States before American fans. But I said that before I was sick.

"I never ever say I'm going to win a race because I know there are too many variables. I've got one of the better track records in the world championship because it really comes down to no outside help. One on one is what the world championship is."

5

A Helping Hand for Others

Pascal Poisson rode for the Renault team with Greg LeMond from 1982 through 1984 and still marvels at his generosity. Like most stars, LeMond shared his prize money with his teammates, but in addition, at the end of each season he gave expensive gifts to the anonymous workers on the team, the mechanics and the masseurs. One year, Poisson says, LeMond gave each of three masseurs a splendid new massage table. "It wasn't just by chance that all the other riders were so happy he won the Tour," the Frenchman says. "He's known for his friendliness and kindness."

PEOPLE LIKE GREG LeMond. They respond to his friendliness, his openness, his ability to remain levelheaded about himself and his accomplishments. "There's no temper, and an awful lot of self-control," said Alexi Grewal, the winner of the gold medal in the road race at the 1984 Olympic Games and a teammate of LeMond's in 1989 with Coors Light in American races. "Greg's always easy to get along with."

Until his second victory in the Tour de France, however, not everybody realized how tough-minded LeMond could be. At the lowest points in his comeback, even when he talked of escaping the pain and humiliation by quitting, he refused to do more than talk about it. Recalling his agony earlier in 1989, he said, "I was planning to stop cycling. I couldn't, but it did enter my mind." As quickly as it entered, he thrust the thought out.

Riders are always astonished by the fragility of their morale. "Without it, cycling becomes too hard," says Ron Kiefel of the 7-Eleven team. "You have to *want* to do it, *want* to live it. Mentally and physically it's just too difficult. If your morale is shot, you can't train, and then you suffer a lot more than you should when you race. It's a terrible spiral if you don't have that drive."

Even as a teenager, LeMond had the drive and tough-mindedness. He likes to talk about his first trip to Europe, when he realized that he could race on better-than-equal terms against the best young riders, and how he ended the trip by going to Poland alone for a race. "It was nearly one trip too many," he said.

Eddy Borysewicz, then the national coach in the United States, was a native of Poland, and during the summer before the 1979 junior world championships he kept encouraging young LeMond to go there for a stage race. After much discussion, LeMond agreed and went with the Gordis family to race in Switzerland, France, and Belgium. Those races over, he began thinking again about Poland.

"I couldn't get hold of Eddy B., but I assumed he'd arranged it," he said. "So I went to Poland carrying a scrap of paper with a hand-scribbled address in Lodz. Another American, Greg Demgen, who had raced with me in Belgium, was supposed to go with me, but he got sick and never showed up at the Brussels airport. With two hundred dollars in my pocket, I ended up going by myself, Brussels to Warsaw, where I found I was about seventy-five miles from Lodz. I sat in the Warsaw airport looking for somebody who would recognize me and take me to Lodz. There I was, an American in Poland, looking conspicuous in the airport with my bikes and suitcases. It was a nightmare. I remember getting a Coke at the bar, walking back to my luggage when the bottle slipped out of my hand and shattered—pow—on the floor. Everybody in the whole airport stared at me. After three hours of waiting, I thought, 'What should I do?' "

Many another seventeen-year-old boy would have tried to take the next plane back to the West, but LeMond seems not to have considered that option. "Finally I got my bags and negotiated with a taxicab driver, showed him the address. He said, 'Difficult, a long way.' He wanted eighty dollars for the drive, but I figured that if I spent eighty dollars, I'd have only a hundred and twenty left for nearly a week there, so I got him to do it for forty.

"We got to Lodz and I finally found Mr. Bek, the national track coach in Poland. He was the father of two guys who were helping Eddy B. coach in America. It was a complete surprise to him and his wife that I'd shown up. I tried telling them that I was there for the race—'Eddy B., Eddy Borysewicz,' I kept saying—and finally they called the organizer and got permission for me to race. Then we drove to the south of Poland.

"I was so depressed. Try to imagine yourself at seventeen all alone in a foreign country where nobody's expecting you. It was only a three-day race and my plane ticket was for a week, so after the race I'd still have four days left there. I wanted to go home so badly, but all I could do was race. I ended up winning a stage and getting third place overall. It was good experience, very difficult racing.

"It wasn't only the racing that was difficult. I don't care for milk, and for breakfast before the time trial that opened the race they gave me a bowl of warm milk with noodles in it. I didn't want to eat it, and a guy who spoke some English said, 'What, you don't like our soup?' He made it sound as if I was insulting his whole country. 'No, no,' I said, 'I love it. I just don't want to eat too much before the time trial.' Then I went out and got second or third place in the time trial."

The parallels between LeMond at seventeen and at twenty-eight are striking: "*All I could do was race.*" What he has usually done in difficult situations is to compete and come up a winner.

As those who have known him for years understand, LeMond is a happy man at peace with himself. Part of this is his upbeat, confident personality. "Basically he's an optimist," his wife says. "He always, always looks at the best side of a problem. Whenever something really bad happens to us, he says, 'Maybe in the end this will work out for the better.' Even his hunting accident changed our lives for the better. A lot of people would get down about such bad things happening, but he'd say, 'Everything will work out in the end, and if it doesn't we'll just change our lives and make the best of it.' "

LeMond's personal life has been full of love. He dotes on the support of his mother and father, the strong bonds between him and his wife, the affection they share for their children. His fulfillment as a professional racer, making him a man happy at his work, spills over into the rest of his life. If he had not made his comeback, those close to him say, he still would have remained essentially happy. He knows himself and has a strong sense of self-esteem, rejecting envy and might-have-beens.

Early in his career, before he first won the Tour de France, LeMond was sometimes criticized for apparently lacking panache—that special flair or showmanship that Bernard Hinault had in abundance. LeMond dismissed these critics. "You have panache when you're the strongest," he said. "When you're strong, it's easy to put on the afterburners and blow people away." He had not been doing that, even though people had been saying for years that he was the next superstar.

"Superstar," he snorted. "That's because Hinault has been saying that. Superstar—but compared to whom? You can't compare me to Eddy Merckx or Bernard Hinault. I'm just Greg LeMond; I'm a different type of rider.

"Hinault has a very strong character. He says he's going to win and sometimes he does win, but I never say it ahead of time. People who don't understand think it's a complex, that I don't want to be first. I don't want to make predictions; if you don't back it up they say, 'He's all talk and no show.' I don't say I'll *win* the Tour; I say that I *hope* to win the Tour."

Both Merckx, a Belgian, and Hinault won the Tour de France five times and dominated professional bicycling for a decade each. "The rider I would never compare myself to is Eddy Merckx, of course," LeMond said. "He was probably the ideal cyclist. I believe that Hinault was as talented as Merckx—physically he was as awesome—but Merckx managed to get motivated for all the classics and for the Tour de France too. Hinault couldn't do that. Merckx was what everybody wanted in a bike rider, and he was perfect for his time. I don't believe we'll ever see another rider capable of winning more than four hundred races."

The reason, LeMond pointed out, is that today's bicycling is much more competitive than during Merckx's time in the late 1960s and most of the 1970s. "Cycling has better athletes than it did then, and the riders' mentality has changed. When Merckx rode, he was the boss and everybody else on the team was his slave. It's not that way anymore. Today, if you're on a team, it really *is* a team, not a collection of guys working for a boss. In the big races, everybody on a team realizes who the best rider is and they work for him, not just for the designated boss. If the team wins, rather than its leader, it's still good for everybody. Only in Italy does a team still ride exclusively for the leader, whether he's in form or not, and that's why Italian teams tend to fall apart when their leader isn't doing well. Nobody else dares try anything and so there's no point in working hard every day.

"With the big money being spent now, no team can depend on just one leader. A team needs a strong rider just for the classics and a strong rider for the Tours. Today it's impossible to build a team around one leader unless he's an Eddy Merckx—and nobody is.

"I'd love to be like Merckx, to have his drive. I realize why I don't: I haven't grown up with cycling. I have a different mentality and way of life. Hinault is like me in that respect; he was brought up a decade after Merckx in a different cycling era. For him the important thing was to win the Tour de France, though of course he wanted to win some other races to prove himself. I share that feeling: I'd like to win a classic someday to prove that I can. But my main priority is the Tour de France. That's not the way Merckx was. He wanted to win *everything*; he wasn't called the Cannibal for nothing.

"Also there's a psychological factor. Athletes perform better in their home country. Merckx was an exception to that rule; it didn't seem to matter much to him if he was riding in a classic at home in Belgium or in Italy or France. The rest of us get an extra lift riding in our own countries. I don't want to race in America, for example, unless I know I can try to win. It's something built into me because I've always won in America. The French feel that way about their Tour. Look at the Italian riders; they're great in Italy, but in France they don't do anything. They're just not motivated. They know it doesn't matter to their sponsors, and they don't feel national pride is at stake. If they're criticized in France, who cares; they don't read French newspapers and their sponsors probably don't either."

LeMond is a keen student of the psychology of the athlete, especially of the American athlete in Europe. "The hardest part is living a different life," he said. "Americans have a tough time dealing with this; they like to be freer. I've never fought the system, but I've never let them push me around either. I'm an adult. I know what I have to do to perform well and I'll train properly. I don't always need to be with the team. When I come to a race, I'll be in good shape. They don't realize that Americans are different."

Understanding this, LeMond has helped young American riders in different ways. An example is Andy Bishop. When he was forced to miss the 1988 Tour, LeMond was replaced on the PDM team by Bishop, who owed his job to the older rider. Two years before, Bishop had been an amateur doing well in the Tour of the European Community, a race for young riders that LeMond had won in 1982 when it was called the Tour de l'Avenir. At the race's farewell banquet, Bishop met LeMond, a guest of honor. "I had an offer to turn pro with a Belgian team," Bishop related, "and I asked Greg—it was the first time I'd ever spoken to him—whether he thought it was a good team for me. He didn't; he said he thought a Dutch team would be better and that he'd ask his team if they knew of anything open. I thought, Sure he'll ask, because he didn't know me from Adam. But a day later I got a call from PDM and a day after that they signed me.

"He's always honest and straightforward," Bishop concluded. "I think he's made a special effort with a lot of Americans because he's interested in helping the sport to grow. He always helps Americans' chances in Europe."

Each year a handful of American riders travel overseas to seek glory and wealth with a European team. Almost unanimously they find European life too demanding, too foreign, and after a season or two they return home.

"Most American riders have different attitudes about racing from Europeans; they're not used to suffering," LeMond explains. "In the U.S., the sport is never hard enough to bring out the best in a rider, so most American riders aren't used to top-level competition and the racing conditions in Europe. For my first two or three years in Europe I always felt pretty tired in races, but that's part of the sport. Those first two years in Europe are the hardest part."

LeMond mentioned an American rider who had failed to stick with his European team. "He wasn't prepared to have to race as a business," he said. "When you're a professional you're supposed to have graduated from that babying stage, taking it easy if you get the sniffles." But the change is vaster than that. "Now I'm used to it, but at first I got crazy when I had to eat the same food for three weeks straight with the team," LeMond continued. "It's monotonous, but you learn to live with it. You learn that it's your work and that's it."

Mike Chavez would not have disagreed about the hardness of his new life. Nothing went right for him in the first two months after he moved from the United States to Italy to become a professional rider. Climate, food, water, culture shock, even the air he breathed conspired to weaken him. "Ever since I've been in Italy I've been fighting illness," he said during a race across Italy in 1988. "In the past four or five days, my stomach has been grinding and I haven't been sleeping well." Trying to find a cure, he was planning to return to New Mexico to see a doctor.

"I've been brought into reality," Chavez said in the hotel where his little-known Selca team was staying during the Tirreno–Adriatico race. The day had been a disaster for him:

starting in 176th place among the 177 riders, he dropped out during the only climb. "It was a hard stage," he said defensively. "They're all hard when you feel bad. The climb wasn't that steep but it was long and I haven't been doing well going uphill ever since I was sick.

"Bike racing is a humbler. Americans say bike racing in Europe is as big as football, or baseball, or basketball but it's actually even bigger, and much harder."

Chavez was full of respect for LeMond and Steve Bauer, the Canadian, who have lasted years on the European circuit. "It's amazing for me to be here with those guys. People don't understand how hard it is to come here and do what they've done. Until you come here yourself, you just don't realize it." But he did not feel awe, he insisted. "They're great racers and they do well but I don't feel there's any reason why I shouldn't do well too." His results in other seasons were good, he pointed out. He began racing at seventeen in Colorado, where he had moved from his native Albuquerque to become a ski racer at Vail. "It turned out I was a better bike racer than skier," he admitted.

In 1984, after racing in Vail, Colorado Springs, Denver, and Boulder, Chavez visited a brother who was stationed with the U.S. Air Force in Kaiserslautern, West Germany, and began bicycling there as an amateur. Three years later, unhappy with his progress in the U.S., he returned to West Germany. "Things were very good for me there," Chavez said. "I raced well and got good results. I'm mostly a sprinter, but in the last year or two I've been able to stay with the climbers."

Word gets around in the small world of professional bicycling. An official of the Ciclolinea Company, which makes cycling accessories, spotted Chavez and recommended him to Selca, for which Ciclolinea is a secondary sponsor. A small, low-budget team that races almost exclusively in Italy, Selca is named after its primary sponsor, a maker of electronic bug exterminators. The team needed another man and the American came cheap.

Chavez also came with immediate problems. "I got really sick—seven days in bed—just before the Giro of Sicily and wasn't able to race at all. The climate, the food, and some water I drank had something to do with it. There was a flu going around and the water made my resistance low, so I was the first to get it. It took its toll: my blood pressure dropped and everything went bad. In Germany I had no problems; here the climate's been very difficult, hot and cold, hot and cold again. Also I'm used to a dry climate and it's very wet here."

Chavez was living in a small town near Bologna, where training was difficult. "The air isn't good because there's a lot of farmland and they burn all their fields off. And all the cars burn gas into the air. It's something you just have to get used to. I haven't adjusted to the climate and living constantly on the road. Every day you race from here to there; you stay in a hotel, then race again and stay in another hotel."

Chavez looked around the dingy hotel on the gray, polluted Adriatic and winced. "Professional racing is a whole different world from amateur racing. You don't just say, 'Okay, I'm a pro now.' There are too many good riders who can win each race."

Was he simply homesick? "I did feel that at first," Chavez admitted. "Just communicating with other people was a big problem at first. Sure, I'd like to go home, but this is what I want to do. Everybody has good days and bad days. I've gotten this far and I'm not going to stop now. I'm planning to go back to the U.S. for a little while and recuperate; then I'll be back." He said this bravely, reassuring himself, unaware that this was what American riders always said before they went home and stayed there.

Upstairs in the same hotel, LeMond was astonished to hear that another American rider was in the race. "Mike who? An American! What's his name?" He thought for a moment, then said, "I've never heard of him." He was not being unkind, merely factual. A careful reader of bicycling magazines and newspapers, LeMond follows other riders and knows their results. In some ways he is still the fan who daydreamed with Kent Gordis and read *Miroir du Cyclisme*, saying aloud the foreign names and conjuring up dreams of glory.

When he heard about Chavez's medical problems, LeMond was solicitous. "The problem for American riders over here is that they're exposed to so many different types of sickness. My father-in-law, who's an immunologist, says there are thousands of types of cold viruses. When you're growing up, you're exposed to most of them. That's why having a cold isn't always bad; your body builds up immunity to that virus. This guy should see a doctor about getting a vaccine, and make sure he doesn't have a stomach virus."

LeMond sat in silence for a moment. He had been down the same path as Chavez, and it awakened memories. "Imagine starting on an Italian team, especially a low-budget one," he exclaimed with feeling. "My God, you're talking about a mean, hard life. If you're Italian it's one thing, but gosh . . .

"I was lucky on Guimard's team," LeMond continued, referring to the Renault team he joined in 1981. "I'd probably do it over again, but now that I know how hard it is, God . . . I was confident of myself, but I didn't really know what my potential was. So many things go into a rider's success. He can have all the physical qualities, but does he have the mental qualities to survive while learning? I was determined; I knew that I was going to make it; I had to. I knew that I had what it took to become a very good rider, but still my first two years were difficult. Some young riders think, I'll just take a pro license out. But it's the hardest sport in the world. The problem with jumping in too soon is that you become demoralized and don't give yourself time to adapt."

LeMond looked around the small, tacky room with its low-watt bulb too weak to read by. It wasn't much but at least it was a single; the day before he had found himself the third person in a two-man room. He seemed to be weighing the advantages of being a racer, especially an American one living in Europe. "It's been so educational," he said at last. "You could never reproduce what I've learned. I appreciate Europe now. I get to see what life is really like in Europe. I like European life—Belgium, Paris, fantastic! I can go to any major city in Europe and find my way around. I'm as American as you'll ever get, but I'm the kind who can go anywhere in the world and not have any problems." The thought cheered him immensely.

At dinner that night in the charmless restaurant in the hotel, LeMond and the rest of his PDM teammates were in high spirits. They were all riding well in the Tirreno-Adriatico race and the outlook was good for the rest of the long season. As voices were raised, noise bounced around the room, and the waiters serving pasta and fish joined in uncomprehending laughter at the team's jokes.

In their corner the Selca team ate silently. Conversation was mumbled and bowls of spaghetti were passed with a grunt. Chavez sat far forward in his chair, ignored. When he had finished his dinner and was heading out of the dining room, eyes downcast, another American intercepted him and brought him over to LeMond. After they were introduced, LeMond promised to see him later. Chavez went out and ordered a coffee at the bar.

After five minutes, LeMond pushed back his chair and made his way there, standing next to Chavez. For the next fifteen minutes, the Tour de France winner and former world champion chatted with the untested young rider while one by one the Selca team drifted past and looked them over. Nobody dared to interrupt.

Finally LeMond shook hands with Chavez and returned to his table in the dining room. A few minutes later, Chavez strolled in; his shoulders were thrown back and he walked with a bounce. He marched directly over to the table where Selca officials, mechanics, and masseurs were still eating dinner, pulled out a chair, turned it around and straddled it, placing his elbows on the table. Then he gave them all a radiant smile.

Chavez was still smiling when he left the dining room and headed for his room upstairs. The next day he was gone, but he had gone happy.

As American as Mud Pie

After Greg LeMond won the Tour de France for the second time and returned to the United States for the winter, the French newspaper L'Equipe *sent a reporter with him to write about the reaction back home. There wasn't much, the journalist's account said. When LeMond went to the White House to see President Bush, not a head turned in recognition as LeMond strolled up Pennsylvania Avenue. Even worse, when he reported at the airport in Minneapolis that a suitcase was missing from the flight, the woman behind the counter never looked up when he gave his name. "How do you spell that?" was all she asked. The Frenchman wrote that LeMond seemed accustomed to this treatment and was not even ruffled.*

DESPITE THE CONTINENTAL capital *M* in the middle of his family name, Gregory James LeMond is as American as mud pie or his favorite Tex-Mex enchiladas. His ancestors were mainly Scots-Irish on his father's side, and English and Chero-kee Indian on his mother's. "Possibly my dad's side of the family is French way back," he says in trying to explain the sound of his name. "The name used to be spelled LeMonde, but they dropped the *e* because in America everybody pro-nounced it 'LeMondy.'"

His sense of being an American, and therefore a curiosity in bicycling, was reinforced throughout LeMond's first years as a professional racer. For many seasons in Europe he was always introduced at races as "Greg LeMond, *l'Américain*" or "Greg LeMond, *el Americano*" or "Greg LeMond, *il Americano*." French, Spanish, and Italian crowds marveled at the rarity of an American competing in what was regarded as a preeminently European sport. Yet late in the nineteenth century professional bicycle racing was a major American sport, rivaling even baseball. "Cycle racing occupies as promi-nent a place in the estimation of the ever-vacillating public as any sport recorded on the calendar," reported *Spalding's Offi-cial Bicycle Guide* for 1898, two years after the Telegram Tro-phy Race in Worcester, Massachusetts, attracted 50,000 spectators. With the advent of the automobile, however, the roads were cleared of cycling races and the sport began to focus on the track, where sprinting and six-day races remained popular for decades. A full racing circuit ranged from Boston and Worcester to Newark, New Jersey; St. Louis, Missouri; Toledo, Ohio; Fort Wayne, Indiana; Des Moines and Council Bluffs, Iowa; Salt Lake City; and San Francisco and San Jose, California.

Then the sport went into such total decline during the De-pression that Americans forgot about it. When LeMond won the Tour de France in 1989, the ABC program devoted to the final stage attracted a North American audience measured at 5 points, more than double most previous Tour programs. Explaining the rating, an ABC official told the French daily sports newspaper *L'Equipe* that though such a rating was far below the World Series or the Super Bowl, it was respectable for "a non-American sport."

LeMond bristles at this attitude, even though he understands it. He remembers that he bought his first bike not to race but simply to get around. When Americans think of the bicycle, they think mainly of transportation, rarely of competition. Cycling is the most popular American recreational sport, with 85 million participants, including 20 million who cycle at least once a week, but the difference between recreational and professional riders is enormous. "Everybody rides a bicycle when he's a kid, and so he thinks it's the easiest thing in the world to do," Bernard Hinault often complains. "Or maybe they still ride on the weekend with their kids or go shopping on a bicycle. That's enough to convince them that they understand racing. Sometimes they might even get rained on before they make it home, so they think they know just how it is for us with a hundred and fifty kilometers to go in rain or snow. If everybody's done it, it can't be very hard, can it?"

Especially since 1984, when U.S. riders won a handful of gold medals at the Los Angeles Olympic Games because such traditional powerhouses as East Germany and the Soviet Union boycotted the event, bicycle racing has been gaining popularity in the United States. The United States Cycling Federation, which governs the sport, often cites the 1984 Olympics as the spark the sport needed to catch fire—an attitude that LeMond contests. "The people there don't understand anything," he complained a few years ago, before the federation changed many of its officers. "My dad was talking to a USCF official who said, 'It's incredible how popular cycling has become in the United States. We've gotten six thousand new licenses in the four or five months since August 1986, and I honestly can't tell you why! I don't understand why the sport is so popular now.' He took no account of my victory in the Tour and how much the publicity about it meant to cycling in America. I believe most of its growth in the U.S. comes from my first victory in the Tour."

Of course college football champions and World Series winners routinely visit the White House, but LeMond was the first cyclist to be received there, after his first Tour victory, by President Reagan. ("He gave Geoffrey some jelly beans.") In September 1989, he again visited the White House and gave President Bush a yellow jersey.

LeMond's anger with U.S. bicycling officials is long-standing and antedates even their opposition, once the boycott of the Moscow Olympics was announced, to LeMond's decision to turn professional. Years later, his usually calm face would turn angry when he thought about their skepticism and obstructionism. In fairness to the officials, he did point out that before him only a few Americans had tried to race as professionals in Europe, and that none had been a champion. Still, years of accumulated bitterness took over as he remembered the clashes with USCF officials at the world championships in Prague and Goodwood, and what he perceived as a lack of respect for his accomplishments. By European standards— ones LeMond is now accustomed to—the USCF was long regarded as a notoriously inept group, divided by internal politics and at best indifferent to U.S. professional riders. "The amateur program in America has people with no knowledge advising it," LeMond complained after his first Tour victory. "Predictably, American cycling officials were upset by my turning pro. Eddy Borysewicz warned me, 'You're going to burn out by turning professional.' Burn out! What I've been burned by is sideline coaches, especially when I was young and much more advanced than anybody else in American cycling. Sideline coaches don't know nearly as much as they think they do. Luckily I had a level enough head to realize that nobody

in the U.S. knew what they were talking about. If I'd listened
to all the sideline coaches there, I'd have stayed an amateur
until the 1984 Olympic Games, which would have stymied my
whole career. I might never have been the cyclist that I am
today. Coaches in the U.S. work at a much lower level than,
say, Cyrille Guimard. They simply don't know what it takes
to make it.

"So I made up my own mind. I honestly feel I've always
made the right decisions for my career. A lot of people said,
'Greg is going to be chewed up by the Europeans. He won't
accomplish anything.' They got it wrong, didn't they?

"But that's the way they think at the top level in American
cycling. Let me tell you about the junior world championships
in Argentina in 1979. It was probably the most successful
junior world championship for an American team ever, and I
don't think we got even a congratulatory telegram from anybody connected with the U.S. Cycling Federation except for
Eddy B. In Buenos Aires we did something that's never been
done in American cycling, and I won three medals. Finally
we're going to get some recognition, I thought. On the plane
back home we all wore our U.S.A. uniforms, and we won-
dered how many journalists would be at the airport and how
big the crowd would be. But at Kennedy Airport only Eddy
B. was waiting for us. Nobody else cared. There were no
journalists, no fans, and especially no USCF officials."

LeMond will not acknowledge it, but he knows that American officials were right to worry about his chances in Europe
at that time. "Finally, though, with the 7-Eleven team turning
professional in 1985 and participating in European races like
the Tour de France and the Tour of Italy, people in the United
States are getting a good view of how hard professional cycling is. I race in Europe because that's where the best competition is; if the best competition was in the U.S. I'd be racing
there.

"Ever since I went to Europe I've been accused of neglecting American racing, but I feel I've been doing more good for American cycling by winning in Europe. I could race in the U.S. for the next twenty years and not do as much good for American cycling as I did by winning the Tour de France. When was the last time you saw the result of a bicycle race on the front page of *The New York Times*?"

Along with any imagined or real criticism in his own country, which became muted after he was shot, LeMond has endured criticism in Europe because of his way of life. Other American riders have analyzed the difference between American and European attitudes, and Ron Kiefel of the 7-Eleven team, who was the U.S. national champion in 1988, sums it up well. "Americans see things outside cycling," he says. "We have a much broader perspective. We think about education and our families. We know that if something happens, we can always go out and get a good job. In Europe it's cycling or nothing; you ride your bike or you go work in a factory or on a farm. They don't go to school and cycle at the same time; they make their choice at a young age."

Family and life beyond cycling concern LeMond, too. "I want to be as successful as I can while still keeping a somewhat normal life," he says. "The way some riders live is not normal. When all you do for twelve years is race, eat, sleep, and then race again, you're missing out on life, and you'll never recapture those years." In his open, easygoing way, he is extremely popular with most other riders, but for a long time he was regarded almost as a dilettante who succeeded because of his vast physical gifts. How well would he ride if he took it seriously? more than one team official asked.

He does take it seriously, LeMond answers. "It makes me bitter to be criticized for not being single-minded," he says. "I've had to sacrifice and dedicate myself to a foreign sport in foreign countries."

LeMond mentioned an article that appeared years ago in *Bicycling* magazine in the United States, comparing him to the ascetic Sean Kelly. " 'If Greg wants to be a true champion, he can't play golf,' " he said, parrotting the criticism. "Those may not have been the exact words, but that was the point of the article—that Greg LeMond doesn't act like a European. But I'm American, and I come from a different way of life. If an American magazine can't understand that, no wonder the Europeans can't either. The truth is that I have a different idea of how I want to race."

Unlike many Europeans, LeMond does not ride six-day races in the winter, participate in all the prestigious classics in the spring and fall, and live in Europe the year round. "It's very difficult for me to race from February to October without a break. I don't think that's unreasonable." His main goal is the Tour de France; after that he often returns to the United States before some major fall races simply because he is burned out.

A major part of the European misunderstanding of him, LeMond feels, is that people do not understand how difficult it is to be riding far from his own country, and how he needs to live occasionally like any American of his age. "I get tired of talking to the same journalists and having them write the same stories with the same criticism over and over again. Like about golf."

Before he was shot, LeMond was an avid golfer, usually shooting in the low eighties. By playing the game, however, he defied conventional wisdom that a rider should stay off his feet when not training or racing. During a day off in the Coors Classic in Colorado in 1986, when American television showed LeMond out golfing, his French teammates were scandalized. After their usual training ride, most of them had spent the rest of the day in bed.

LeMond makes it clear that he golfs to relax, not because

he is not dedicated. "You can't have won the Tour de France, the Super Prestige award, and the world championship without training hard. Those victories didn't happen by accident; I worked hard for them.

"I've lived my life the way I wanted to and I've been criticized for it, but I'm happy, and that's what's most important to me. If I golf in Belgium during the season, I'm doing it because I know it's not going to affect my cycling. What it boils down to is that my priorities are a little different from, say, Sean Kelly's."

LeMond chose the right man as contrast. In a now-classic story, first told in the book *Kelly*, by the Irish journalist David Walsh, after a race in the Netherlands Kelly's wife, Linda, was sitting on the hood of the family car, waiting for her husband. When she got down, she left a mark where her hand had rested, and Kelly wiped it away without a word. Mildly annoyed, Linda complained that her husband's priorities were first his car, then his bike, and finally his wife. As Walsh wrote, "Kelly heard the accusation, turned and with a look of deadly seriousness told his wife that she had gotten the order wrong: 'The bike comes first.' "

"That's the kind of mentality I have to fight in Europe: that bike racing is the top priority," LeMond said. "When I was shot there was a big scandal about my going hunting. Instead of people asking, 'Is he going to live?' they said, 'Greg should never have been out hunting.' Those people are so callous. If I'd been racing the Tour of Italy and had a disabling accident, that would have been okay; I would have been hurt in what the writer considered the line of duty. But hunting, no!"

LeMond is also troubled by his reputation as a businessman in a cyclist's shorts and jersey. He and his father have capitalized on his victories as no other rider has; there is no Team Hinault selling bicycles as there is a Team LeMond, and few other riders have moved from team to team, putting together ever more lucrative contracts, as often as the American has in the last few years. "Greg is a nice boy and a good rider," said an official of one of his former teams, "but it was sometimes hard to believe he was concentrating on riding."

Again LeMond feels that the best defense is a good offense, and he bristles at the critics. "Everybody thinks Americans are hard businessmen: we demand this, we demand that, the Europeans say. They think it about me especially. But they forget about the demands they put on me because it's convenient to do so.

"Most riders are developing a more professional attitude. They're realizing that their careers can be very short, that cycling doesn't last forever and that money is a major factor. But none of them want to admit it. That's the difference between me and European riders. They know deep down inside that they're racing because they're trying to make a good living, as well as because they like the life. You couldn't do something this hard if you didn't like it.

"I came to Europe to win the Tour de France, but I also knew that I was a professional, and in order to live and survive, I had to act like one. If I talk to a team about a contract, I've got to be prepared, because those guys on the other side of the desk are businessmen.

"When I started cycling at the age of fourteen, it was purely for fun. After I started winning all those races I got my first real sponsor. At seventeen I had an introduction to the business side of the sport far in advance of most European riders. They don't see the business side until they turn professional, which in most European countries isn't until a rider is twenty or twenty-one years old.

"Two facts color my attitude about the business side of cycling. First, my early experiences here, and second, the fact that I'm from a country where sports are big business. Even in Europe, however, everybody on the business side of sports treats it like a business, though they won't admit it. The reason people pay part of your bills when you're an amateur and pay your salary when you're a professional is not because they love you or respect your ability or want to help you do well in the sport. No, it's because cycling is a *business*, and that's the lesson I've learned.

"Most sponsors—and I've seen this ever since I signed my first professional contract with Renault—are really in it for the short term, eager for as much publicity as they can attract in three years and then getting out. That's why I tell riders that though they might have a strong sense of loyalty, the sponsors rarely have that feeling for them. When they want to drop the sport and put riders on the unemployment list, they go ahead and do it. When they want to ignore what your contract says, they do that too.

"Despite the moves I've made from one team to another, all my dad and I have ever done is to try to look out for my best interests. This sport is notorious for treating riders badly, and when I first came to Europe I was shocked by how people treated me in business."

LeMond looks back to his early years to make his point about sponsors. He started with Renault and stayed with it from 1981 until 1985, when he moved to La Vie Claire, also based in France. In 1988 he moved to PDM in the Netherlands, and in 1989 to ADR in Belgium, which shared his contract with Coors Light in the United States. He left each team with some acrimony.

"When Renault negotiated, it was always me against six or eight executives intimidating me—or trying to—by telling me that I had to sign the contract. 'We're giving you so much more money than anybody else that you can't let this get out.' The point was to keep it quiet so that nobody would know the kind of money I was making. But you wouldn't guess how big this staggering sum was that the Renault executives wanted to keep secret. When I first went to Europe I signed for six thousand French francs, about twelve hundred and fifty dollars a month. That's fifteen thousand a year in 1981, not so very long ago. Yet they acted as if it was double what somebody else would get. You wouldn't want to stir up the boys by admitting that you were getting all of twelve hundred and fifty dollars a month, would you?

"Still, I jumped at the offer. I was there by myself against a whole table lined with executives, with Guimard off to the side, and I talked to my dad on the phone. The decision had nothing to do with money; we were certain we wanted to go with Guimard. I didn't know much about him, but I had heard that he was Hinault's coach, and it was after I talked with him that I decided."

At the same time, LeMond was approached by Peugeot, then one of the leading teams in France, with a long tradition in the sport and a roster full of other young, English-speaking riders. "But I knew there was no way I wanted to go with Peugeot because I'd heard that the team was lenient about using drugs," LeMond recalled. "To this day I don't know whether that was true, but it was a rumor going around then. There were plenty of others about Peugeot. It was a bad-reputation team, and my dad and I were convinced that between the two we wanted to go with Guimard. He had coached Lucien van Impe to victory in the Tour de France in 1976 and then developed Hinault, who won the race in 1978, 1979, and 1980. We were impressed that Guimard had refused to let him ride the Tour in 1977, when he was twenty-two years old, because he felt that Hinault wasn't ready for a grind like that, even if the French people and press were convinced that he should be in the race. Guimard seemed to be a coach who protected young riders.

"But Peugeot kept trying to get us to sign with them. I'd been offered six thousand francs by Guimard but—and I want to repeat this—I didn't really care what the money was. Everybody forgets that. My main objective was getting the right team and right coach so that I could develop. In the long run, I felt I was going to make more money, but that would come later.

"In 1980, the year before I signed with Guimard, I made thirty thousand dollars from sponsors and prizes racing as an amateur in the U.S., so I was going from thirty thousand dollars a year to fifteen thousand with Renault, a sizable pay cut. I felt it was worth it because Guimard was such a good coach and would develop me into a top rider.

"But Peugeot couldn't be turned off. First they offered me ten thousand francs a month and then fifteen thousand, more than double Renault's offer. Finally, my dad and I told them, 'You'll have to offer twenty-five thousand francs a month to have us even consider going with you.' We weren't saying that to bargain; we were just trying to discourage them. Five thousand dollars a month was about what a top star like Hinault was probably making. I gave them a number so outlandish that I was sure they'd leave me alone."

As LeMond admitted, the plan backfired. "Peugeot spread the word that Greg wanted the world. It's a reputation I still haven't been able to shake."

The Million-Dollar Man

When LeMond won the world championship in 1982, the townspeople of Kortrijk planted four flagpoles in his front lawn, running up the flags of Kortrijk, Flanders, Belgium, and the United States. Four years later, a group of fans camped in front of the house from the Sunday that he won the Tour de France until he returned home well past midnight on Tuesday. They had painted on the pavement the greeting "Champion of Champions," and later that day the mayor gave LeMond a gold medal. The fans were back in 1989 in nearby Marke, but this time there was no gold medal, just cheers and celebrations.

AT HIS HOME in Kortrijk, Belgium, in June 1984, Greg LeMond was looking ahead a bit to his twenty-third birthday, but as usual was not expecting much of a celebration. "His birthday's always a dud," Kathy explained. One problem is that he is apt to be away at a race, and this time was no exception, though he would be returning home late that night.

It could have been worse. "One year we were in Hamburg and the only thing we could do to celebrate was to go to a fast-food place and have two or three beers," LeMond said. But he refused to be drawn into any speculation that a special present he could give himself that year would be a victory in his first Tour de France, which would begin a few days after he turned twenty-three. The time had finally come to enter the world's greatest bicycle race; he was world champion and had won such prestigious multi-day races as the Coors Classic, the Dauphiné Libéré, and the Tour de L'Avenir.

His Renault team thought highly of LeMond's chances, but he was careful to play them down. "I'm going to do as well as I can. If I don't succeed this year, I've got five or six more tries." He thought about this for a few moments, and then his voice grew stronger. "Of course I'm shooting for victory," he admitted. "If you don't, why race at all? You don't ride the Tour for the experience."

Leaning back on his living room couch, LeMond seemed relieved by his confession. Still, victory seemed not to be everything to him. He said he much preferred the method of Bernard Hinault, at that point a victor in four Tours and a strong favorite in the coming one, to that of Eddy Merckx, the Belgian who had won five Tours a decade earlier.

"Hinault picks his objectives. He doesn't try to win everything. I'm not a cannibal like Merckx. In the past, riders sacrificed their health and longevity to win everything and to race from February through October. I think you've got to rest and recuperate between races."

Both LeMonds were happy to be living in Belgium. About five miles inside the country from the French border, Kortrijk is the sort of town where the main square is sometimes closed to traffic in the summer so that people can nurse a beer at an outdoor café and listen to a band concert. It had other advantages too; "Everybody in Belgium speaks English," LeMond noted. His French was getting more fluent, "but it's pretty dirty because I learned it from French racers." The television set in a corner of the living room brought in fifteen channels, including the BBC and a subscriber service from across the Channel that printed the news, including sports, on the screen in English.

At that time the LeMonds lived in a quiet street with a suburban air, renting a gray-brick two-story house with a small lawn in front and a big backyard. Inside, the house could have belonged to any young American executive. The books were by Le Carré, Forsyth, Clavell, and Ambler.

A couple of years later, the LeMonds bought a house in the nearby village of Marke. Home was again on a quiet suburban street ("You don't need to lock your car") in a two-story white stone house. The purchase had worked out well financially. "I bought it when the dollar was at its highest." He laughed boyishly, pleased by his bargain. "We wanted something we could really enjoy because we spend so much time here. Kathy is here eight months a year. Earlier in my career, I thought of our life here as temporary, but now I realize that we'll be here for a while."

In both houses there was barely a hint that LeMond was a professional racer except for a pile of team jerseys next to the washing machine, some bicycling magazines under the coffee table, and a small photograph on the mantel showing LeMond, in a business suit and tie, surrounded by an Italian youngsters' cycling team; the photo was inscribed in respect and gratitude for his appearance with them. Like most well-known athletes, LeMond is in great demand. "Everybody wants to claim you," he says, "to invite you to dinner or to a party. We usually have to turn them down. If I did even half of what I was asked, my cycling would go downhill."

LeMond talked offhandedly about being a celebrity. "I told our neighbors we might be moving closer to Antwerp, mostly for the bilingual schools, when the baby begins going to school. They said, "No, no, you can't." It's not that I'm famous here, but a lot of people know who I am."

LeMond was often greeted by total strangers, he said, when he rode along the Kortrijk canal on the way to his daily training route. "It takes about two or three minutes to get out of town on a bike. You can never get into the real country in Belgium because it's all villages, but I head toward the hilly section of Flanders. I try to stay out for four or five hours a day, which is about a hundred and twenty to a hundred and fifty kilometers."

The Tour was occupying LeMond's thoughts, of course, and he kept a map of the course close by his seat. "It will be a very difficult Tour," he said, "very mountainous, but if I'm a hundred percent and feel good, it should suit me."

Riding for Renault, LeMond was planning to share leadership responsibilities with Laurent Fignon, who had won the 1983 Tour when their team leader, Hinault, could not start the race because of surgery for tendinitis in a knee. "You can always use two leaders, at least for the first week," LeMond said. "Then we'll see who's in the best position. I know I'd work hard for Fignon and I think he'd work hard for me."

A few months before, Fignon said publicly that he thought LeMond would eventually leave Renault to make more money. At the time LeMond seemed surprised by the prediction. "The only way I'd leave Renault would be if a big American team came to Europe and I was at the end of my career." But as it turned out, LeMond was wrong and Fignon right, changing the face of professional bicycling.

Little in that 1984 Tour went right for LeMond, who was troubled first by a cold, then by a sore throat and problems with his feet. With a week of the race to go, he was unhappy. "I'm not quite myself yet and Fignon is above the rest of us." Indeed he was, breezing through the Alps with two victories, a second place, and a fifth place, as he opened a lead of more than nine minutes over Hinault, who was now riding for the Vie Claire team. "I've ridden eight Tours, including all of Hinault's wins, and I've never seen anybody do what Fignon is doing," said Sean Kelly. The Frenchman finally cruised into Paris a winner by 10 minutes 32 seconds over Hinault as LeMond finished third overall, 1 minute 44 seconds behind Hinault. As debuts in the Tour go, LeMond had done well, even winning the white jersey of the best young rider, but he had certainly not fulfilled his hopes. Worse, he was no longer a co-leader of the Renault team with Fignon, who had now won the Tour two years in a row.

LeMond was brooding about his diminished role a few weeks later when he let it be known that he had been approached by "a big French team" to sign a contract. Barely a month later, the news became official: La Vie Claire, headed by Hinault on the bicycle and Bernard Tapie at the cash register, announced that LeMond would join them in 1985. The price was astounding. At a time when Hinault was probably making $200,000 a year and the average rider $15,000, LeMond had agreed to $1 million over three years.

"Maybe a lot of people felt I got paid too much to sign with La Vie Claire, but I felt I deserved it," LeMond says defensively. "I thought it was a fair price, and everybody out there now is making a lot more money because of my contract with Tapie. Before I signed with him, I'll bet there was only one rider making over two hundred thousand or two hundred fifty thousand dollars a year, and that was Francesco Moser in Italy. Now twenty or thirty riders are making a lot of money, thanks in part to me, and yet I'm the only one who's ever criticized for being interested in money."

When Tapie first announced the contract, LeMond denied that a deal had been reached. "I'd like to stay with Renault," he insisted, "if they offer me the same kind of deal. But if it doesn't work out with Renault, I'll go with Tapie."

Renault was paying LeMond about $100,000 a year, plus such perks as his rent, a couple of company cars, and eight round-trip airline tickets to the United States. With fees for criteriums, he was believed to be making $350,000 a year, including endorsement fees, the heart of his troubles with Renault, he said. As he was to do in later years when he changed teams, LeMond bitterly accused Renault of breaking promises to him. "They've let several companies abuse my name," he said. "I've got lawsuits going against five companies because they say I endorse their products—brakes, saddles, all the components. Renault promised they'd help me fight this, but they haven't done a thing."

LeMond denied that he was joining La Vie Claire because of any unhappiness with his teammates, especially Fignon. "Fignon and I are good friends," he insisted. "It's the best team in the world, and Cyrille Guimard is the best coach in the world. I've got a lot of friends there, but the way La Vie Claire is building itself, it may be the second-best team around." Formed late in 1983 after Hinault quit Renault in a clash with Guimard, La Vie Claire was then a pet project of Tapie, a French businessman who grandly announced that he intended to drag professional bicycling into the twentieth century.

"I remember the first time we met, during the Tour in 1984 on an off day in the Alps," LeMond said. "He came up to me and asked, 'How would you like to make a lot of money?' We went on from there. Tapie seems much more professional to me than most of the businessmen and sponsors in cycling. I mean it as a compliment when I say he seemed much more American about business. That's the way American business-men talk: 'You want to make a lot of money, we want to make a lot of money.' "

When he enticed LeMond away from Renault, Tapie said about the million-dollar contract, "If he weren't an American, there would have been a zero less." The remark was generally interpreted as a reference to Tapie's business interests in America, but Tapie said later that he was misunderstood. He was referring to the bargaining tactics of LeMond's father. "Contrary to what has been written, we had no international aim, no world economic vision," the entrepreneur said in an interview in his spacious office in Paris. "We wanted only to build the best team in the world. Our goal was victory, so we went out to look for the best riders without paying any atten-tion to their nationality. If the best had been French, we'd have had an all-French team. But they weren't, so we have Swiss, Danes, and Americans too. If I'd needed to recruit a Martian to win, I'd have done so. Greg cost a lot, but he was the best available."

At that point, early in 1986, or a year after he signed LeMond, Tapie was sounding disappointed in his recruit. "I'm not unhappy with Greg," he insisted. "He is among the five best cyclists in the world. But he is missing that little bit extra to make him number one. He has class, he has the will, the physical tools, the team, but he must take the initiative. As long as he doesn't, he will not be a leader. He has never been the boss, and he still doesn't realize that the boss is the one who says to his team in the morning, 'This evening, when the race is over, I'll be the winner.' That's what he's missing.

"Second, third, second, third—his record is full of those finishes," Tapie grumbled. "Second place is the same as twenty-fifth place." In life as in racing? No, Tapie did not go that far. "Fortunately, life is not about winning," he explained. "Life is about happiness, and we all have that capacity. But we can't all win the same race. There are ten cyclists on a team, but only one can win. So for the others to accept him as a leader and be willing to fight for him, Greg must win."

Describing LeMond variously as nice, a true professional, courteous, and unpretentious, Tapie insisted that relations between them were good. LeMond begged to differ. The honeymoon was over and he would acrimoniously leave La Vie Claire—or Toshiba, as it was renamed for another of Tapie's French companies—the year after he won the Tour de France. "The reason I quit is simple," he said. "They didn't pay me on time. They didn't keep their promises. They didn't treat me with respect."

The whole fuss sounded familiar, LeMond admitted. "I came into a lot of the same kind of criticism about being money-crazy when I left Renault at the end of 1984. Sure, I got a revolutionary contract for a million dollars spread over three years, plus an option year. What Tapie offered me was a really good contract at the time, but why shouldn't it have been? It was the correct figure for my value.

"Even so, I could have avoided a lot of bad press if Tapie had cooperated. I had asked him to keep the amount secret. Fat chance of that when he saw an opportunity to zing the cycling establishment and to get lots of publicity while doing so.

"Guimard tried hard to keep me at Renault. I remember sitting in a hotel room with him just after we finished a stage near the end of that Tour, and Guimard said, 'Greg, you've been sick. You were on antibiotics for fourteen days, you raced this Tour on one leg, and still you're going to finish third. I promise you that if you stay with me you'll win three or four Tours.' Can you imagine hearing that when you're twenty-three years old and for years have dreamed of winning just one Tour?"

However, LeMond reasoned that Fignon would be a major hurdle to his own ambitions. "We were the same age. I just couldn't imagine being allowed to challenge my teammate, a winner of the last two Tours, in the next one. On the other hand, La Vie Claire's leader was Hinault, who was much older than me and on the downslide. I didn't realize that he was going to come back, and I thought it would be better to ride with Hinault on Tapie's team. But of course money had something to do with my decision as well. Renault was paying me a hundred thousand dollars a year and Tapie had offered to triple that, so I had to tell Guimard, 'I want to stay with you but I can't ignore this kind of money. It's my whole security, and there's no guarantee that I'll win the Tour.'

"I was so right about guarantees. You never know what's going to happen. The following year, Fignon was out with tendinitis in a heel and needed an operation.

"Renault didn't want to release me because I had a contract for the following year, an option year for both of us, but most teams won't keep you if you're unhappy. At the Tour of Holland in August, a week before the world championships, Tapie let it be known that I'd already signed with La Vie Claire. I hadn't, but that was Tapie's way of putting pressure on Renault and getting me in trouble, hoping they'd agree to let me go. I didn't know this was going on, and still wasn't entirely sure I wanted to go with La Vie Claire. At the very least I wanted to give Guimard a chance to make a counteroffer. But Tapie forced the issue, which he likes to do. Then, right after the world championships, I sent out a press release that Renault had written, denying that I had signed a contract with La Vie Claire. It was true; all I had done was make a tentative agreement to come to La Vie Claire. You can't legally sign a contract until October, and this was early September. Tapie knew all this, but he continued to force the issue by announcing that I'd signed for three years for $1 million. What a stir it created!

"It was typical of Tapie; he wants publicity. He's a funny guy, with lots of charm and personality when he wants to show them. In 1984 he was just another businessman in France, though admittedly a pretty big one. He jumped into cycling with a splash, promising that he was going to be a savior of the sport and really promote it, which for me proved to be a mixed blessing. He did help the sport, and he's done a lot of good, but not all that he promised.

"Am I bitter about Tapie? I guess the answer is that I'm not bitter, but that I am disappointed in him."

LeMond's mixed feelings about Tapie are most obvious when he discusses their negotiating sessions. "This is where he's at his best. He's very convincing, a dynamic person, a good personality when he's trying to acquire you. Once you've signed it's different. In 1986 he told me, 'The reason I don't like you, Greg, is because you come in here with your dad and you ask for different things. Bernard Hinault is the best guy for me because he doesn't give a damn. He sits back and he says, "Oh, you give me this—all right." ' That's easy for a sponsor to work with.

"When he left Renault in 1983, Hinault was making a hundred fifty thousand dollars. That's after winning four Tours and the world championship. The guy should have been making at least five hundred thousand a year. Hinault's attitude is what all sponsors want: 'You give me a contract; I'm happy just to ride.' I've always approached it differently. My dad and I feel that we offered La Vie Claire and Tapie a service. It's a business. The feeling Tapie gave me was that when they paid me, that was that; I was a hired hand and no more. I felt that if I went downhill, they'd get rid of me as quickly as possible—no sentiment, no loyalty, no respect. The reason he wanted me was to sell bicycle pedals in America, and that was it. They had no intentions of trying to support me; it was simply a business relationship. I want more than that with an employer or sponsor; if I give my personal loyalty, I want some in return.

"Tapie always says, 'Whenever I talk to Greg, we only talk about money.' What does he expect? He was my boss, and he's so busy that it never occurred to me to call him up just to chat. Also, I really don't know him well enough to call him just to chat. He's right when he says we only talk about money on the phone: the only time I've had to call him was when I was six weeks late in getting paid. I've got bills to pay, and banks and people are pushing me and my dad to get paid.

"When I joined La Vie Claire, the sky was the limit, at least in promises. Tapie said, 'We'll spend a million dollars promoting you in the U.S. This was while he was wooing me away from Renault. He said, 'I own the Toshiba franchise in France, so you can get all the stereo equipment you want. We'll give you first-class airline tickets when you fly back and forth, and your salary will only be one fourth of what you'll earn.'

"I think Tapie had good intentions, but most of it was the art of negotiating. We got the first-class airline tickets, after a fight; the agreement was in writing. But when I got the contract, somehow they'd forgotten about the airline tickets, everything. It was all just promises."

When he left Tapie after the 1987 season, LeMond agreed to join PDM, a team based in the Netherlands. "Moving to PDM was a whole new lease on life," he said. "I was convinced they would be a pretty good team when I got back on top. I knew that when I left a French team for a Dutch one, the French press wouldn't treat me nicely. Okay, I can accept that and not worry much about it. What I did care about was

how the French public reacted; that was a major consideration in my thinking, because that's where the Tour de France
is and I want the French people to like me. I like them; most
of them are very sportsmanlike and fair. If it was up to the
public, they would cheer on the best riders and that would
be that.

"Many people assume I went to PDM for a big pay raise,"
LeMond continued. "They're wrong. It was a slight one, but
I have a bonus system where I can make more by doing well.
But I could have gotten that from any other team. I told PDM,
'You're the team and organization I want to go with because
if we have the right riders, we'll be one of the best teams.' I
want to get back on top without pressure. If I'd gone with an
Italian team, they'd have paid me double, but if I didn't do
well they'd nail me.

"I was offered six hundred thousand dollars a year, and I
turned it down to take considerably less from PDM. People
think I'm in it for the money, but I think I deserve the
money that is correct for my market value. I don't chase the
dollars; if I did, I'd be racing six-day races in the winter, and
criteriums. I could make three or four hundred thousand
dollars a year extra that way. Instead, my main goal is to
excel in the Tour de France and live a life that has some fun
in it. I don't even keep the prize money I win in races; I give
it back to the team. We put all our prize money into a pot
and divide it by the number of days we've raced at the end
of the season. That's the best way to keep up team morale.
Only a few riders can do really well, but the rest realize that
if they really support those riders, they're going to make a
lot more in prize money.

"Team support is more important to me than anything extra
I could make for myself. I'm not greedy. I don't have to kill
myself in criteriums and six-days. The most I ever did was

fifteen or twenty criteriums in 1981, the first year I turned pro, because I was making only fifteen thousand dollars a year. Now I don't need that money. I have my health. When I'm finished with cycling I don't want to be afraid I'll die at the age of fifty from a heart attack. It's not a healthy sport; it's too difficult.''

8

Hinault's Prisoner

At the end of 1989 Bernard Hinault talked with the French magazine Miroir du Cyclisme *about his relations with Greg LeMond. Looking back nearly a decade to their first days as teammates, Hinault said, "Above all, it was his determination that impressed me. I give a lot of importance to determination. If you have all the physical gifts but not conviction and perseverance, there's no hope." When it came time in the interview to discuss the 1986 Tour de France, Hinault was unapologetic. "I kept my promise to help Greg win the Tour by riding the race I had to ride." He did not elaborate.*

OFFICIALLY THE 1985 Tour de France started in Brittany on the next to last day of June, but symbolically it began in Paris early in February 1983. On that day, in a restaurant in the Bois de Boulogne, the Renault team presented its riders to the press. This was still the era of Bernard Hinault as the leader of a collection of unknowns, a point underlined by Renault's little joke of having all the riders troop onstage wearing papier-mâché Bernard Hinault masks.

There they stood, fifteen clones, one by one lifting the masks as each rider's name was called and his achievements listed. Marc Madiot, Charly Bérard, Pascal Poisson, Laurent Fignon, Vincent Barteau, Maurice le Guilloux—and finally it was Greg LeMond's turn. In those days he knew little French, and when the announcer introduced "the winner of the Tour de l'Avenir, the American," LeMond didn't pick up his cue. In the pause that followed, Hinault walked over, flipped up the mask, and smiled indulgently at the young man behind it. Liberated, LeMond blinked at him.

So it was in the 1985 race itself, with the avuncular Hinault in full command. As a vast crowd of his fellow Frenchmen lined the Champs-Elysées, he won the Tour de France for the fifth and, he said, last time. He was planning to retire at the age of thirty-two after one more season, and his last year, he said, would be spent in helping LeMond—this time with the Vie Claire team.

"Greg knows he can ride for victory next year in the Tour," Hinault said just after the 1985 race ended. "I'm just planning to have fun and make some trouble in the next Tour. All I want to do is help one of my teammates win. If all goes well, that should be Greg LeMond." This time, instead of blinking, LeMond exchanged a beatific smile with his leader.

Hinault's fifth victory equaled the record set by two of the sport's greatest champions, Jacques Anquetil and Eddy Merckx. Anquetil had won his Tours in the late 1950s and early 1960s, and Merckx dominated the late 1960s and early 1970s. His retirement ushered in the era of Hinault, who won in 1978, '79, '81, '82, and '85.

Hinault won the 1985 Tour by 1 minute 42 seconds over LeMond, almost always a willing prisoner of his team and his loyalties. Third overall, 4:29 behind, was Stephen Roche, an Irishman, with Sean Kelly, another Irishman, fourth, and Phil Anderson, an Australian, fifth. When Hinault mounted the victory podium his face bore few signs of the fatigue and injury that had marked it since he'd crashed in a sprint finish midway through the race, breaking his nose and cutting his scalp. "Except for the fall," he said, "this would have been an easy victory. LeMond's support really helped. Because he was there, I was able to relax."

A long scar on the inside of his right knee was the only trace of the surgery that had kept Hinault out of the 1983 Tour and limited his power in 1984, when he'd finished second and LeMond third behind Fignon. "I have something to prove," Hinault insisted before the start of the '85 race, which Fignon missed because of similar surgery for heel tendinitis. With Fignon out, Hinault was confident: "Look at the final results last year Fignon first, me second. Now Fignon won't be there. Draw your own conclusions." Was he being arrogant? "If I sound sure of myself," Hinault answered, "it's because I am."

At the opening of that season Hinault set his and his team's goals: victory in the Tour of Italy, the Tour de France, and the world championships. "After that," Hinault said, "I am at Greg's service." There was little reason to doubt the pledge, since the two riders had long been friends, with Hinault seeming to fill the role of older brother to LeMond. All season long, as the designated heir, LeMond had been the most faithful of lieutenants, first helping his leader win the Tour of Italy, while he himself finished third, and then supporting him in the Tour de France.

Only once did the Hinault mask slip from LeMond's face. After his fall in St.-Etienne, in which Hinault and Anderson collided with 250 meters to go, the Frenchman announced to his teammates, "I still have my two arms and my two legs, and

I'm far from being dead." Still, he had trouble breathing and showed signs of physical distress in the Pyrenees. In the climb there to Luz Ardiden, LeMond opened a lead on Hinault that he mistakenly believed put him in the race leadership—what the riders call the yellow jersey on the road, a fanciful and far different matter than the actual yellow jersey that the leader dons at the end of each daily stage. Scenting the real yellow jersey, LeMond began to press ahead to widen his lead, but his team car drew alongside and he was ordered to slow down and assist the struggling Hinault. More precisely, LeMond was told not to help Roche, who was with him on the climb. LeMond obeyed and finished only a minute ahead of Hinault.

Furious afterward, he accused La Vie Claire officials of not having allowed him to win. He was called in for a conference with Bernard Tapie. When he emerged from the talk, the American was contrite. "I got a little carried away," he said, explaining that when he had said, "This was my chance to wear the yellow jersey, one of my dreams," what he really meant was that he would have done so only for one day before allowing Hinault to reclaim it.

Throughout this flap, LeMond and Hinault did not criticize each other. "There hasn't been any trouble between Greg and me," Hinault said. "What was important was that one of us win. Greg did his job and I did mine, and the result is that we're one-two in the race. Greg didn't really understand what was happening. He reacted like any young, ambitious rider; he spoke from the heart, and that showed his virtues. He has a lot of character."

Character was also Hinault's forte. He seemed genuinely pleased when LeMond beat him by five seconds in the final time trial to record the first stage victory by an American in the history of the Tour. "I'm as happy for him as if I'd won myself," Hinault said. The Vie Claire team manager, Paul Koechli, put the stage victory into broader perspective.

"We've just seen a true passing of power," he said. "Greg showed he's ready to take on all the responsibilities of a team leader. Who could have hoped for a prettier end to this race?"

The time-trial victory was not only LeMond's first in two Tours, but also his first major success since he'd won the world championship in 1983. "I've been wondering when it was going to happen again," he admitted. As the American nodded in confirmation, a teammate, Bernard Vallet, said, "I think this victory was very important to him because he was beginning to develop a complex about not winning. This sets him free."

Vallet, who had turned professional with Hinault in the 1970s, also had an interesting comparison to make between the present and future team leaders. "Bernard is above everybody else," Vallet said. "He astonishes me with his resources. He's more sure of himself and of his strength than he's ever been. He may not be as good as he used to be in the high mountains, but he knows how to be at his best exactly when he needs to be. That's what they mean by class." Then he spoke of LeMond. "Greg has the class to win the Tour, but I don't know if he's hungry enough. He doesn't have Hinault's destructive rage, but he doesn't have his single mindedness either. He's a lovely boy, but certainly too kind."

Koechli, the Vie Claire manager and strategist, worried about that kindness too. Early in the next season, LeMond was riding in the Paris–Nice stage race and hoping for a good showing to establish his leadership. "This team has been built around working for the strongest rider," he said at the breakfast table. Ahead of the riders lay 150 kilometers and a climb up fearsome Mont Ventoux, with lunch only the standard bag of sweets, fruits, and small sandwiches to be eaten as the riders pedaled along. "In the major races you have to take the attitude that you're going to be the best rider and hope that the team helps you. This team is a lot like Renault. We have the same principles: there are leaders, like I'm the leader today because I'm the best-placed overall. But if today I have a bad day and somebody else takes the lead, he'd be our leader. We're not like some teams, where even if there's a stronger teammate, the leader still calls the shots."

Koechli had been working to reassure LeMond. "This is Hinault's last season," he pointed out, "so it's a transition year. Bernard is still riding and is a great rider. It's up to Greg to impose himself. He's got to take the reins. Sometimes he still seems timid."

It was a strange word to use for a rider as aggressive as LeMond, but it may have been accurate. The American is a nice man—perhaps, in those years, too nice. "Sometimes, maybe," he agreed. "Sometimes in a race when the team's not doing well, when our riders aren't at the front, I have a hard time shouting 'Get up here.' Hinault would just yell at them."

Even while speaking English, which was unfamiliar to most of his teammates, LeMond took the precaution of lowering his voice when discussing leadership. He did not make trouble.

He knew, LeMond continued, that some riders on the team were "a little more loyal to Hinault. But that's only natural; they've raced with him for ten years. Then there's the language. I can't really communicate that well with the French riders. I can talk to them, sure, but I can't tell them *exactly* what I mean."

The year before, Hinault and LeMond had parted on splendid terms. The sports newspaper *L'Equipe* ran a cartoon as the Tour de France ended, showing Hinault with a bicycle and LeMond pedaling a child's scooter; the Frenchman was saying, "Because you've been so good, I'll take you along next year on my handlebars." To which LeMond replied, "Thanks, Uncle Bernard."

Uncle Bernard? A year later, the morning after his own victory in the Tour, LeMond admitted that he was weary. "I'm still feeling the effects of the pressure," he said. "Then when the race was finished, they whisked us around from one ceremony to another. After that we had the team party and"—he nearly yawned—"it was five A.M. when I got to bed. So I've only had three hours' sleep." Through the fuzziness, one moment stood out for the American victor in the world's greatest bicycle race. "It felt good to have Hinault congratulate me on the podium in Paris after everything that had passed between us."

The remark said a lot about the 1986 Tour. Since LeMond had finally won the big one, the victory he had craved since 1984, why did this personable and balanced young man seem so unsure of himself? The answer lay in the games Hinault had played with him. "The real conflict was between me and Hinault," LeMond judged. "He wanted to win the Tour and so did I. It was a delicate situation."

Indeed it was. Despite his public pledge not to ride for victory but to help his teammate win, Hinault began to hedge as the 1986 race approached. Once it started, he went for victory—not to set a record of six triumphs, for Hinault is sincerely uninterested in records, but because he was unable *not* to try to win. Even LeMond, who felt betrayed, could acknowledge that Hinault had not acted out of malice, but simply had been unable to restrain himself from seeking victory. In the end, as he said, he helped LeMond win, though he chose his own peculiar way of doing it. Peace broke out with only three days left in the twenty-five-day race, when the Frenchman called off a series of physical and psychological challenges to LeMond, ranging from taunts to audacious breakaways designed to give Hinault such a lead that LeMond would be reduced to the role of support rider that he filled the year before.

To use the riders' term for it, Hinault dynamited the race. Knowing that the mountain stages were the most formidable in at least a decade, he set such a rapid pace on the flat for the eleven days before the mountains that the best climbers were burned out. Then when the pack reached the Pyrenees, he dashed off again. "The climbers have nothing left, no reserves of strength," Hinault explained. "You've got to attack them until they can't recover. That's not hard to do." In a race that was expected to be dominated by climbers, the highest ranking at the end in Paris was the unsung Samuel Cabrera, a Colombian who finished eleventh overall, more than 35 minutes behind. "This was my fourth Tour and by far the hardest," said Robert Millar, a Scot. "It was awful on the flat as well as in the mountains. I don't think we've ever climbed the Alps and Pyrenees so fast." Millar did not finish the Tour, but Hinault did, second overall and winner of the polka-dot jersey that goes to the king of the mountains.

Hinault's tactics were widely celebrated as a sign of his panache, a quality the French revere. In his daily column in *L'Equipe*, Anquetil wrote, "This Tour was fantastic, and we owe it all to Hinault. Even if he didn't win, it was his greatest Tour de France."

In a country that adores a winner, Hinault had never been an authentic hero. Outspoken and often belligerent earlier in his career, he had mellowed enough to make his famous promise to LeMond, but as the American pointed out, referring to the 1985 stage in the Pyrenees, "Everybody forgets that Hinault might not have won last year without my help." His public promise had created a no-lose situation for Hinault. "If he wins a sixth time, he'll be a hero," said Anquetil. "But if he makes LeMond win, he'll also be one. In either case, the fans will love him."

They did. Everywhere along the route the French public cheered Hinault, especially after he won three daily stages to become the second-biggest stage winner in Tour history. Hinault finished his career with twenty-seven stage victories in the Tour; only Merckx, with thirty-four, did better. Part of the reason for Hinault's popularity was recognition that a page was being turned: of all French riders, he seemed to be the only one capable of winning the country's major race. In 1985, LeMond had already symbolized the ascendancy of both English-language and young riders in European racing. Aside from Hinault, Kelly, and Anderson, none of the first ten finishers in the 1985 Tour was more than twenty-five years old, and five of them—LeMond, Roche, Kelly, Anderson, and Steve Bauer—speak English. Four others—Pedro Delgado and Eduardo Chozas, both Spaniards, and Luis Herrera and Fabio Parra, both Colombians—speak Spanish. In 1986, two Americans—LeMond and Andy Hampsten—finished in the first five. Internationalization of the sport, the great dream of the race's organizers in the 1980s, had come with a vengeance.

If Hinault could do no wrong for the French, the cheering for LeMond was still warm. He rode with less flair than Hinault but stayed with him, and then ahead of him, throughout. The pressure was all on the American, not on Hinault, who could say, "This Tour has been an enormous pleasure for me because everything revolved around me. I said at the start of the year, 'I'll pull the strings in the Tour. I'll play with the others.'"

As the American rider Alexi Grewal characterizes him, "Hinault is the psychological master of all time, the guy who could bluff the best." Grewal meant the description to be both admiring and critical.

"Bernard Hinault has a double personality," said a man who knew him well, Michel Laurent, then an official of the Vie Claire team and formerly a rider who competed against him.

"There's the rider and there's the everyday man. After his evening massage, he's relaxed and easy to live with. But the racer is always looking for motivation, and most of the time he finds it by being aggressive. He always needs to boost himself up over somebody."

In 1986, that somebody was LeMond. He won just one daily stage, a grueling climb in the Pyrenees to Superbagnères, but it was supremely important since it was the day Hinault tried to open such a huge lead that LeMond would have been forced by team strategy not to attempt to regain his deficit. The Frenchman went off alone on a breakaway the day after opening a nearly five-minute lead on the American with a similar attack. On the evening of the first breakaway, LeMond said forlornly, "It looks like I'm going to finish second in the Tour again." Twenty-four hours later, he was elated, having recovered nearly all the lost time, and winning the stage when Hinault ran out of power on the last climb. As he had so many times in the race, Hinault justified his attack by saying, "Even if it didn't work, it helped Greg, didn't it? The most important thing is the team's victory."

LeMond continued to finish high regularly: first and third in the Pyrenees, second and third in the Alps, second to Hinault in two time trials. He was proud of his consistency. Excluding his time-trial victory in the 1985 Tour, he still had not won a major race since the world championship in 1983, but had done so well overall that he was second in the International Federation of Professional Cycling's computer rankings of the world's best eight hundred racers. Hinault ranked fifth on the computer but first in the war of nerves that rattled LeMond just before the Alps. After the Frenchman went off on another breakaway, LeMond caught him, but then threatened to quit the race. "Hinault's forgotten his promise," he charged.

"What's his trouble?" Hinault replied disingenuously.

"Are his legs hurting? Maybe it's just as well that he quits if he doesn't want to win the race anymore."

The next day, on a climb in the first day in the Alps, LeMond took the yellow jersey back from Hinault, dropping him into third place behind Urs Zimmermann of Switzerland. At the finish line, noting that he was now 2 minutes and 43 seconds behind the American, Hinault complained of soreness behind a knee but insisted that he was by no means ready to concede the race. "He looks cute," he said of LeMond in one of those comments open to many interpretations. "Yellow looks good on him." LeMond had no response to such remarks; sometimes he simply smiled at the barbs, or else looked dazed. Like anyone attacked from an unexpected quarter, he appeared confused and hurt.

Despite the trouble with his knee, Hinault looked fit the next morning as the riders prepared to tackle the climbs over the Galibier pass and up to Alpe d'Huez. He showed exactly how good his form was by storming down the 2,460-meter Galibier with Zimmerman, Bauer, and Pello Ruiz-Cabestany, a Spaniard, the four of them overtaking the first two men at the peak, Herrera and Guido Winterberg, a Swiss. Riding hard, LeMond joined the group. It was a great moment for the Vie Claire team, which had four men—Hinault, LeMond, Bauer, and Winterberg—at the front. Herrera was first to be dropped, Winterberg next, then Zimmermann. Bauer was shed at the start of the next climb, up the 2,067-meter Croix de Fer, and Ruiz-Cabestany soon afterward.

For the remaining seventy kilometers, this was one of the great afternoons in racing history: Hinault shepherding LeMond, champion and protégé reconciled, teammates together at the front of the pack as they effectively ended the Tour de France for all their opponents. Hinault led LeMond through most of the descent from the Croix de Fer pass, and then appeared to pace him through the twelve kilometers and twenty-one hairpin turns up to the resort of Alpe d'Huez, opening a five-minute lead on Zimmermann, who chased alone. Near the top, with victory certain, LeMond pulled alongside his teammate and, before hundreds of thousands of spectators, threw an arm around him as Hinault broke into a huge grin. Overall, Zimmermann was 7:41 behind and Hinault 2:43 behind; despite the week to go, LeMond appeared to have won the Tour.

Just before the finish line, Hinault raised both their hands in triumph, but LeMond slowed and allowed the Frenchman to have the stage victory. "By finishing hand in hand," Hinault said later, "I think we gave a wonderful image of what sports are all about."

It was a joyous, emotional moment for everybody who saw it, a reconciliation, a healing. But it was a sham.

"I really thought that after Alpe d'Huez, I would ride into Paris with the support of the team," LeMond said. Instead, ambition still burned within Hinault, and he quickly returned to his war of nerves. "I'm very proud of what we did together," he said at a press conference the next morning, "but let me say it one more time: the Tour isn't over. Who was stronger in the climb? Go on, ask Greg." At his side, LeMond merely smiled.

Hinault said it would come down to the final time trial at St.-Etienne, a slightly rolling fifty-eight-kilometer course with a small hill near the end. The time trial was scheduled four days before the end of the Tour, and a day before the final mountain stage, up the demanding Puy de Dôme. The Frenchman offered his version of peace: "In no case will I attack Greg at Puy if I haven't won back the yellow jersey before then." This promise was extracted by Bernard Tapie at LeMond's insistence and threat to stop riding.

At St.-Etienne, Hinault rode a superb time trial. Julian Gorospe, a Spaniard, had the best time in the individual race against the clock, 1.17:37, until Hinault came in an astonishing 2:01 faster. Just behind him was LeMond, the last man to start. He crashed when he took a corner too fast, and later had to change bicycles because the spill had damaged his brakes, but he still managed to finish only 25 seconds behind Hinault, a bravura performance.

That night, LeMond raged with frustration. Conciliatory with the French press, he was blunt with an American journalist, to whom he denounced Hinault. "He made promises to me he never intended to keep. He made them just to relieve the pressure on himself. I just wish he had said at the beginning of the Tour, 'It's each one for himself.' But he didn't, and so I rode one kind of race. If he'd said, 'It's every man for himself,' I'd have ridden differently. I have bitter feelings about him."

Though he did not hear these words, Hinault seemed unconcerned by the growing turmoil. "I've really thrown everything at Greg in the last forty-eight hours," he admitted. "I've pushed him as hard as I can and spared him nothing—not words, not deeds—and have put him under maximum pressure. If he doesn't buckle, that means he's a champion and deserves to win the race. I did it for his own good. Next year maybe he'll have to fight off another opponent who will make life miserable for him. Now he'll know how to fight back."

Would Hinault keep his promise and not attack again? He did. The Puy de Dôme was a quiet stage, with LeMond finishing 17th, 52 seconds ahead of Hinault in 34th place. "That's it," Hinault said. "If I'd won back 2:42 at St.-Etienne and he'd held the yellow jersey by just one second, I still wouldn't have attacked him." On the last day, traditionally a cruise into Paris, LeMond was part of a group spill. Hinault, who had avoided the crash, waited for him. The Frenchman started and finished the day 3:10 behind, in second place.

•   •   •

Their troubles continued a few weeks later when LeMond and Hinault rode in the Coors Classic in the western United States, mainly Colorado. "He was paranoid that I was going to do the same thing to him that he'd done to me, but I didn't care about winning the Coors," LeMond remembers. "After all, I'd just won the world's greatest bicycle race. Still, I wanted to finish high and collect points for the Super Prestige competition, the unofficial world championship.

"In the Vail–to–Copper Mountain road race Hinault beat me by forty seconds, though I still had an overall lead on him. The following day he joined a breakaway and I let him go, so that he was three minutes up. The day after, a rest day, I played golf, driving a cart, and Hinault told the press that a true professional doesn't play golf on a rest day. But after eighteen holes of golf I did a training ride. Of course you can't do that in the Tour, but the Coors isn't so hard, and for me golf is relaxing. If you take a cart and don't walk, it's rest, so his criticism made me mad."

The next day LeMond tried to move up from third place to second, and seemed to attack Hinault. "He was infuriated," LeMond says. "He started crying, got off his bike, threw it down, said he was going to quit, and accused me of riding against him. I tried talking calmly; I said, 'Bernard, you're paranoid if you think I'm doing what you did to me in the Tour. You're overreacting.'

"But he got madder and madder. He yelled for half an hour and wouldn't talk to me. The next day before the start I said, 'Bernard, no matter what you think, you're in the lead because I'm letting you be in the lead. Since it's your last stage race, I'll work for you from this point on; I'll stay by your side and do nothing but ride for you.' Then, since we were so angry at each other, I added, 'That's a promise, which is something that you can't keep.' I said it right to his face."

LeMond kept his word and Hinault went on to win the Coors Classic, the final triumph of his career.

"That's the way our friendship ended," LeMond concludes. "I made every effort I could in the Tour and every effort I could in the Coors to make things right between us, and it didn't matter. It's sad! We raced for five years together, and now everything is so petty. When he retired in the fall of 1986, I didn't go to his party, not just because I wasn't around Europe but because I didn't want to see him again."

The loss of a hero is never easy to understand, particularly since Hinault denied that they were enemies, continuing to insist that he had acted on LeMond's behalf during the 1986 Tour. "I gave my word to him that I would work for him, and that's what I did," the Frenchman wrote a few years later in his autobiography. "It wasn't my fault if he didn't understand how I lead a race. What I did, I did only for him. How dare he say he didn't need me to win? I spent all my time wearing out his opponents. Throughout my career I worked hard for others without having the kind of problems I had with him. Greg LeMond still has to learn the hardest lesson: humility. Humility is difficult for Americans. It seems to me that they aren't bent in that direction."

As a close friend of the Frenchman said, "Hinault is torn between feeling that he threw away his sixth victory and knowing how enthusiastic the fans are about what he did. He's very sensitive to that. He really enjoyed that Tour. In Pau, the evening he took the yellow jersey, he said to me, 'The others rode with their jaws dropping and I was being cheered.' "

Hinault would not have another chance at that sixth victory. True to his word, he retired on his thirty-second birthday in November 1986. The celebration, which he had helped plan for a year, lasted the whole Sunday before his actual birthday.

"It's not a funeral procession," he insisted beforehand, "just a big party." Festivities included a long spin for nearly two thousand cyclo-tourists, who rode through the town of Yffiniac in Brittany, where Hinault was born; a concert; fireworks; a cyclocross race; and a display of the many jerseys, pennants, plaques, and ribbons Hinault had won, including the red buttonhole ribbon of a member of the French Legion of Honor. During his career Hinault had won more than two hundred fifty races, and the exhibition of his victory jerseys included five yellow ones from the Tour de France, three pink ones from the Giro d'Italia, two green-yellow ones from the Vuelta d'España, the red-and-white striped one from the 1986 Coors Classic, and the rainbow-striped one from the 1980 world championship road race.

Thousands attended the farewell celebrations, but LeMond was not among them. "Are you kidding?" he responded when a friend asked why he had not been there.

Even today LeMond has not forgiven his former idol and mentor. When they crossed paths during the 1989 Tour, LeMond was, as the French say, "correct" toward Hinault, now an official of the race among other jobs in his retirement, and the proud Frenchman was equally reserved. They will never be reconciled. LeMond would have it no other way.

9

Twenty Minutes from Death

The long scar on Greg LeMond's stomach is still an angry red against his pale skin. Because they wear short-sleeve jerseys and shorts reaching to the mid-thigh, professional cyclists all develop what used to be known as farmer's tan. In uniform they seem to have been baked brown by the sun until they pull off their jerseys and stand bafflingly vulnerable in secret paleness. With LeMond the surprise is twofold: the pale skin and the ten-inch scar the length of the stomach, where the surgeons had to cut him open to save his life. A few days after his operation, a visitor asked him for a message for his fans in Europe. "Tell them I'll be back," LeMond replied. "I don't know when, but I'll be back."

SINCE HE AND his parents were trapshooters and he himself had hunted as a boy, Greg LeMond grew up around guns. "Shotguns," he explains, "never pistols, which I consider dangerous. I feel safe around guns because I know how to handle them. I've taken hunters' safety courses and always been open-minded about guns, except for pistols. I believe in gun control because as far as I'm concerned, pistols are for nothing except killing people. Anybody who registers a gun is in it for sport."

When he was a boy in Nevada, LeMond often hunted pheasants and, since there were a lot of them around his home far out in the country, quail. "That's the best bird to hunt," he says, "because they're incredibly fast and very tough to shoot. I've never hunted them with dogs, but just by walking up on them. If they're not hunted all the time, quail are pretty nervous birds and they'll flush themselves. A pheasant will sit, just sit, until it gets really nervous, and then take right off. Usually you have to wait and wait, and then they jump up. Once in a while you practically step on them before they take off. Pheasant you get by two or three people walking real slowly, and at the end of a row of corn they take off."

LeMond was talking months after April 20, 1987, when he was shot. He recounted his experience as a hunter coolly, as if to defend himself against accusations that he hadn't known what he was doing on that fateful day when he stalked wild turkey. He was home then because he had broken a bone in his left hand during a fall in a race in Italy. Hunting during the bicycling season was unprecedented for LeMond; heretofore he had been limited to the off-season, from October or November through January. Going with friends, he usually traveled then to South Dakota to hunt pheasant. "They're good eating," he said. "The most I hunt these days is maybe five or six days a year. A lot of my friends are hunters too, and it's a great way to get together. We usually stay at a motel. I used to camp out all the time, but I'm getting soft now—spoiled or soft, I'm not sure which."

He has hunted deer only once, when he was fourteen years old. "I've never forgotten it," he says. "I woke up at four A.M. to go out and look for one. I walked two or three mountains behind our house, all alone, saw a buck, took one shot, missed it, and decided that I didn't really want to hunt deer. Don't ask me why; I'm still not sure why I quit after one shot.

"When I got home it was about eleven A.M., and I'd walked a long time and was exhausted. My dad asked if I'd like to bike with him up to Lake Tahoe, which was forty miles away. I had just started cycling, and didn't know yet how hard it can be. But I wanted to get some training in, so I said, 'Sure.' We hopped on our bikes and went up the mountain and, God, I got tired. I bonked—that empty feeling racers get—and approaching Lake Tahoe, only about half a mile from my dad's friend's house, I couldn't go on. I don't remember whether I started crying, but I got off my bike and could barely walk the last half mile. Never in my life have I been so tired, and that was the extent of my deer hunting."

Still, when LeMond went hunting with his brother-in-law he was an experienced hunter. "But he wasn't. He'd had very little experience—maybe been out once or twice—and even I had never hunted wild turkey. After I was shot, some people thought I was hunting out of boredom while recovering from my broken hand. I *was* bored, I admit that, but that had nothing to do with my going hunting. I couldn't golf, couldn't really do anything for six weeks except train on my bicycle. I'd been riding the bike every day, not doing anything else because of the hard cast I had on my left hand."

One of his father's brothers lived in Lincoln, California, near LeMond's rented home in Rancho Murieta, an enclave of luxury houses built around a golf course and lake. His uncle's property, about forty-five minutes by car from this home, was a favorite place of his to hunt quail. "But there was turkey on the land too; I'd seen some the year before. My uncle was keen to go turkey hunting, and he'd been asking me the whole six weeks I'd been home. I kept putting it off, saying I'd do it the next week, and pretty soon it was almost time to return to Europe. So it wasn't at all out of boredom, but just to get together with Uncle Rod before I went back. It was three days before I was supposed to return."

LeMond invited along Pat Blades, his brother-in-law and a contractor, who was planning to build a new house for him and Kathy in Rancho Murieta. "When I packed that morning for the hunt, I took my bike in the car with me. The plan was to hunt that morning, do a training ride home, and then see my doctor in the afternoon to get the hard cast off my hand.

"We got up to the property about seven-thirty A.M. and made almost no plans about how we were going to get some turkey. We just decided to head up a hill with berry bushes and trees, about three hundred yards from the house. It's a farm of rolling hills, with lots of birds on it. We split up, with my uncle going to the left, my brother-in-law to the right. We had agreed to walk really slowly, sit and wait, then walk further and sit to see if we could spot anything.

"It's very difficult for me to remember exactly what happened, but I remember Pat whistling, trying to figure out where we were. He wasn't sure of my location. Berry bushes are pretty high; besides, we were camouflaged in army fatigues. In turkey hunting, you've got to be camouflaged or the birds will spot you. We also had net masks.

"I remember hearing Pat whistle trying to figure out where we were, but I didn't respond because I thought that if I could understand his whistle, surely the birds could, too. Then he stopped whistling for a while and I remember getting up; I was going to stand and see where everybody was.

"That's when I got shot. The movement did it. He saw that movement in the bushes and reacted. I was crouching and just starting to get up when I was shot. I had only two pellets in my backside; if I'd been standing up straight, I'd have had more. I got it all in my back.

"At first I wasn't sure what happened. When somebody else

is shooting at a target, it sounds as if it's some distance away, but when Pat shot me, it sounded as if my own gun had gone off, even though he was twenty-five or thirty yards away. Any closer and I'd have been dead.

"I couldn't figure out what had happened. My first realization that anything had happened was that I saw there was blood on the ring finger on my left hand. Then I felt numbness. When you get shot you go into shock instantly and don't really know what's going on. I must have tried to stand up again, and I almost passed out. I tried talking, but my right lung had collapsed and I could barely breathe.

"Oh my God, I thought, I've been shot. I tried to say, 'Pat, Pat, I've been shot.' Then I started panicking. Pat said, 'What happened? What happened?' and he ran down and saw me. At first he was calm. I was in such shock that I was saying, 'I'm going to die' and 'I won't see my wife any more' and 'I won't be able to race any more' and 'We were going to build a house, we won't build it now.'

"Everything passes through your head. 'My God, my life is going to end,' I said. That really got to Pat, and he went into shock himself. I can understand. After all, he'd shot his brother-in-law, and then he starts thinking about all the pressure that would come down on him because he shot Greg LeMond the cyclist. Once I calmed down and help came, I felt worse for Pat than for myself."

LeMond's uncle came running once he heard Blades screaming. "They were trying to figure out how to lift me up but I said, 'Just go get the ambulance.' They were both screaming and yelling so much that it made me start thinking, and I screamed back, 'I'm going to die if you guys don't calm down.' So my uncle ran down and called 911 to ask for an ambulance. Then he came back and they tried lifting me, but my whole right shoulder hurt too much, so I said, 'Back up your truck.'

"It took my uncle about twenty minutes to get back to the

house, call for the ambulance, and then back up the truck. Pat said, 'It doesn't look so bad. There's a little blood coming out, but it's going to be okay.' I felt as if I was losing everything. If somebody's shot, you think that they must be in pain. I *was* in pain, but your body takes over and you really don't realize how much it hurts.''

Blades and his uncle tried to lift him, but LeMond said, "It's better to walk out." Another uncle, one who lived on the farm, came and the two of them shouldered him to the truck. "I walked there and then sat for about twenty-five minutes, just waiting for the ambulance. What we didn't know was that an ambulance, a fire truck, and the police were all up at the top of the property because a gate was locked and they couldn't figure out where I was. Finally we drove up there. They laid me out on a stretcher, took my blood pressure, gave me an intravenous, and cut open my shirt.

"All I could think was, If we drive to the hospital, I'm never going to make it. Then I saw this helicopter; luckily it was from the California Highway Patrol. It dropped down and they wheeled me over and I got in. That's when I started calming down and the pain really set in.

"Boy, was I lucky! The helicopter took eleven minutes to get to the hospital at University of California–Davis, which specializes in gunshot wounds and other traumas. They've got a team of surgeons there full time, ready for anything. An ambulance would have taken me to the nearest hospital, which would have been Roseville, a bumpy thirty-minute drive. I could have died because it would have taken longer and I wouldn't have been in a trauma hospital.

"Here's how lucky I was: the helicopter came by pure chance. They just happened to overhear on the radio that a guy had been shot, and they were debating between going to a car accident—a minor one, it turned out—or coming to me.

They were over Roseville at the time; if they'd been over Sacramento, further away, they wouldn't have come. As it was, they saved me twenty minutes, and if I'd been out there another twenty minutes I probably would have died. At the hospital one doctor told me later that I was within twenty minutes of bleeding to death. It was very, very close.

"At the hospital, I started calming down and thought, Maybe it's not so bad. I didn't think it was superficial but now that I was at the hospital, I felt reassured. Then I heard the doctor yelling instructions, and I thought, Maybe this is serious. They rushed me into the emergency room, and a nurse kept asking my name and address. I could barely talk, because my punctured lung hurt so much. Now I realize that she probably did it to keep me conscious and alert, but at the time I got angry at having to repeat Greg—G-R-E-G—LeMond—L-E-M-O-N-D—745 Anilo Way, Rancho Murieta, California 95683. I could barely speak, but I said it three or four times, gritting it out. Finally when she asked me again I said, 'Dammit, Greg LeMond, 745 Anilo Way, Rancho Murieta, California 95683, and don't ask me again!'

"I'm not sure whether this was before or after they put a chest tube in me, which was crucial because of my collapsed lung. They gave me a local anesthetic and put a chest tube in, just pushed it in. I remember arching my back, coming off the stretcher. It hurt so much! They gave me something to calm me down but they couldn't give me any painkiller because they had to figure out everything that was wrong. I remember going under and then waking up in the recovery room. Oh, and I also remember them sponging me down and cleaning me up in the prep room before they put me under. I went into surgery at about nine-thirty A.M. and came out at two-thirty P.M.—that's what Kathy says—but I didn't come to until midnight."

LeMond and his wife were in the spacious, high-ceilinged living room of their rented house in Rancho Murieta, and their son Geoffrey was playing in a sandbox just outside the back door, not ten yards from the communal golf course. It seemed an ideal place to live, but it contained too many bad memories for the family, who had decided not to build there. As LeMond sat in an easy chair, his wife was on the telephone to Minnesota, where they were negotiating to buy a house on Lake Minnetonka. Now she finished the call and picked up the story.

"When I walked into the recovery room you groaned, and I knew that deep down you knew I was there," Kathy said. "I had gone into labor by then and had to go to *my* hospital, but they said I could see Greg when he came out of surgery. I walked in but they weren't ready for me yet. People in recovery are bare naked, completely exposed, so they can see you and they had just lifted Greg up to change the sheets. Out of every single hole in his body he was dripping blood. It was just like a colander. I asked, 'Are you sure he's going to be all right? He has all these holes in him.' He had sixty holes and he was just dripping blood out of every single hole. I was so happy to see him alive."

LeMond nodded and resumed his account. "Then the ordeal of pain began. I started having spasms the next day. My right shoulder was the most painful. I didn't even realize that my whole right arm, including the fingers, was numb until four days later. The tip of my left ring finger was shattered; the doctors didn't know it was broken until five days later. Their main concern was getting out the pellets. They had to remove them from my liver, kidneys, and intestines. There were seven pellets in my arm, and I took some others out myself. About thirty are still there, two in my heart lining but most in my back or legs. The doctors say there is no danger

Being treated for foot problems on the '84 Tour.

With Geoffrey, aged one, at home in Belgium in 1985.

Changing bikes after a crash in a Tour time trial in 1986.

On the victory stand after winning the 1986 Tour. Hinault is to the left.

Covered with mud in the Paris-Roubaix race.

The racer's life. Changing equipment on a brief visit home.

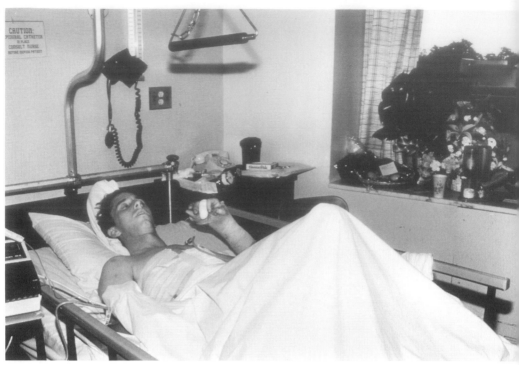

In the hospital a few days after the hunting accident.

An early ride on his bicycle in California after the shooting.

In the Alps.

Seconds before the start of the final time trial
from Versailles to Paris.
Note the triathlon handlebars.

At the moment of realizing that he has won the 1989 Tour.

With Geoffrey, aged five, a few minutes later.

On the victory podium with Laurent Fignon.

Winning the 1989 world championship a few weeks after the Tour (second from the left).

in leaving them there. Your body just forms scar tissue and there is no blood circulating around the lead.

"Because of the pain I was getting morphine shots every four to six hours. A shot relieves the pain, but it's dangerous because morphine is a muscle relaxant and it can stop your heart and lungs. It's great for the first two hours, but then it starts to wear off and the pain increases. They decided to use an epidural on me. They stick it in your spine and give you an injection of morphine. It numbs the nerves all the way down.

"But in that trauma center 90 percent of the people there are from Folsom Prison or are drug addicts, and most of them want drugs to feel good. I think that most of the nurses there were conditioned to believe that maybe I just wanted the morphine to feel good. I kept saying to one nurse, 'I don't believe this epidural is working; I'm in too much pain.' She asked, 'Where is the pain between one and ten?' I said, 'It's a twelve.' She kept thinking I was joking; she said, 'I know you're not in that much pain if you can joke with me.' "

Finally, Kathy's sister Mary, a doctor, persuaded an anesthesiologist to come up from the emergency room at midnight. "She realized that the epidural really wasn't working. I had spasms and my temperature control wasn't good: I was cold, hot, cold, hot. I was naked with a tube here, an IV there, and every twenty minutes they came to take my blood. After two days they couldn't find a vein to stick me in because I'd lost so much blood that the veins had collapsed. And I was having pain and kept saying, 'I can't believe you can't give me something better and stronger.'

"The anesthesiologist thought that maybe the epidural had twisted, or else there was a block in the tube or in my spine. Mary suggested a treatment where you administer morphine to yourself, and it started helping. I still had incredible pain, but the new treatment was just enough to make it bearable.

I was crying because I was in so much pain. If I coughed, it would go on for twenty minutes because I couldn't control it.

"I was in the hospital six days altogether, and this went on for four or five days. I might have stayed a couple more days but in cases like that they want you to be as active as you can. I don't believe the doctor and the nurses understood the severity of my accident. They thought I was lazy, that I didn't want to get up. They didn't seem to realize that for me to walk ten feet to urinate was like climbing a mountain pass in the Tour de France. Harder even!

"The pain persisted after I came home; in fact it didn't end for three or four weeks. I'd sit at home in a chair shaking with pain, sweat running down my face. I'd just cry and cry because it hurt so much. Maybe we should have had a nurse come home with us, but Kathy, her mom, and my mom all took care of me; somebody was with me twenty-four hours a day. I spent four weeks going from my bed to a chair—no more than that—and after four weeks, I was motivated to try more."

Kathy LeMond waited until her husband finished and then spoke softly. "The accident made us realize that nothing is forever. The day it happened I had just finished talking on the phone to Paul Koechli, the manager of Greg's team; we were leaving for Europe in two days, and Greg would be racing two days after that. I telephoned his aunt's house to tell him about the call, and they were still out hunting. Then, two minutes after that, the phone rang with word that he was shot. We didn't know if he'd ever ride his bike again, if he was even going to live.

"Two weeks before the accident we were driving home one night and I said, 'You know, it's almost like we're too lucky. We have everything. Everything's good. We've got each other, we've got our son, we've got no money worries.' Everything just seemed too good. In a way it's good that this happened. Now we appreciate everything more. We learned something from it—that you've got to make every day count."

LeMond said forcefully, "It's not as if I learned that I should never hunt during the racing season. There are lots of accidents hunting, but statistically there are many more deaths in bike riding. It just makes you realize how fragile life is. Everything can be going perfectly, and then suddenly—boom— you're dead! A lot of European sports journalists would like me to change—not hunt any more, or play golf during the season, and just ride my bike. But the accident is exactly the reason why I won't dedicate myself to anything but cycling for the next five years. Of course I want to be successful and I do whatever it takes to make it in cycling. It's not as though I'm not dedicated. I train as hard as anybody in the world, but I have different priorities. The accident has made me realize that a healthy family is the most important thing in the world to me. It gave me time to reorganize my life, and find out what's really important to me. My philosophy hasn't changed, but now it's been strengthened: I'm simply not willing to devote my life a hundred percent to cycling. That isn't the only priority.

"This accident has allowed me to spend much more time with my family. Without it I would never have seen the birth of Scott, would never have helped Geoffrey catch his first fish. I've become Geoffrey's dad; before that I was Daddy, the bike racer. For seven years I've spent half the year away from home, living out of a suitcase in hotels, and the accident gave me time to know and be with my family."

10

Coming Back from Nothing

*Rare is the autograph collector to be turned down by Greg
LeMond, who often shows up late at the mandatory sign-in before
each day's race because he has been waylaid by people with pen
and paper. He often chats with his fans as he signs, but
sometimes, engaged in another conversation, he will absently take
the proffered piece of paper and scrawl his name. One day during
the 1986 Tour, LeMond was explaining his tactics to a group of
reporters when a latecomer walked up, carrying his notebook.
Without missing a beat in the conversation, LeMond snatched the
notebook from the startled reporter's hand and signed it.*

WHEN HE REMEMBERS the early part of his recovery, Greg
LeMond talks first about the psychological pain. Throughout
his career he has cooperated with reporters, answered their
endless, repetitive questions, allowed them into his hotel
rooms and even his home for interviews. He does this because

he is sincerely cooperative and friendly. But now he was shocked to learn that nice guys can finish last.

"I was very upset when I heard what some European journalists had written about the shooting," LeMond says. "That same year a Belgian rider and a Spaniard were killed in races, and the journalists said that this was okay; they'd died on their bikes. But when I was shot and almost died, I got what I deserved. I'm not kidding you; they complimented those guys as if they'd died nobly for some cause, but I got what I deserved because I shouldn't have been hunting.

"One of my bitterest memories in cycling is when I was criticized early in 1987 for stopping a race in Spain. I did so not because of the cold or snow but because of safety reasons. The promoter threatened to try to have me suspended for a month. This was the same man who was criticized for the death of the Spanish rider because the race wasn't safe enough for the riders. The day before I stopped, there were four crashes because of incompetent police. There were two inches of snow on the ground, we were still far from the finish, it was getting late, and everybody stopped. There were four of us in the front, including me, and twenty riders five minutes behind. I said, 'If everybody's stopping, the race has ended.' The organizer panicked. 'We have sponsors and a big crowd at the finish,' he said. I told him, 'We have our lives.' Who knew how long the police would be at the finish to control the crowds and cars?

"In the Tour of Switzerland in 1986, a car ran right past the police motorcyclists and plowed into the front of the pack. Three guys were hurt badly and about a dozen riders were knocked down. The riders wanted to call the stage off, and we did stop for a while so that the injured riders could be helped, but the organizers insisted that we finish the race. I managed second place, but nobody really cared who won or lost. It was just awful that the race continued.

"Some accidents are inevitable; we all know that. Only the really big Tours can close all their roads to traffic a couple of hours before the riders come through. Even in Switzerland, they close only one side of the road. But the attitude that the riders shouldn't have anything to say, that we should just go out and do our jobs without complaint, is simply wrong."

LeMond admitted that he had mixed emotions about cycling after he read newspaper reports of his accident. "I didn't care if I ever raced again. I could have lost everything from this accident. We don't have many money worries, but I'm not so financially secure that I'll never have to work again once my career is over.

"That was the tough part psychologically. Physically it was just as bad. When I left the hospital, it seemed as if every journalist in Europe was here, waiting for me the day I got home and expecting a four-hour interview. Nobody recognized the gravity of the accident; people thought that I'd been shot and then recovered, just like that. The wounds covered such a large part of my body that I didn't have any energy at all until five weeks after I got home. I did see a few journalists because they had flown from Europe; had they been from a local paper, I would never have done it." He smiled ruefully, knowing in his heart that he would have.

"I had no energy," he continued. "I lost fifteen pounds in the first week and a half. My major accomplishment when I got home was pacing in the house about twenty feet. That was major exercise for the first two weeks. It took three weeks after I got home to walk a little more than two blocks."

By the end of May, five weeks after the accident, LeMond started fly-fishing in the lake at Rancho Murieta. "I felt the need to be outside. I'd gotten so used to leaning over that I couldn't straighten up. After fishing for fifteen or twenty minutes my back would be in a knot. I was afraid I'd stay like that and wouldn't be able to ride again. But six weeks after the shooting, I started riding a bike about five kilometers just to stimulate the muscles and keep active. That was the main concern of my doctors, that I stay active.

"After about four weeks of training I started to ride a mountain bike for fifteen or twenty minutes a day, real easy. Then the week before we went to Montana on a family vacation, I did two or three rides that lasted forty-five minutes to an hour. That was my first real exercise, but the effort was low-key. I debated taking the bike to Montana, and in the end I brought it along. Physically I was ready to start training again, but I don't think I was ready mentally, so the bike sat in my travel bag and I didn't ride at all.

"I'm glad I didn't. We rented a motor home and stayed in it and in motels; it's the only way to travel with kids for two weeks. Two weeks with kids in a car gets really old, doesn't it? We went all around southwest Montana and Yellowstone Park. I started feeling good again, and all I did was fly-fish. I was up at seven or eight A.M. and fly-fishing till eleven o'clock at night. It was the right kind of exercise just before I started real training on the bike because it got my body and stamina up to normal. By the end of that trip I felt normal again. It took me about two months just to get back all my blood." (He lost nearly two quarts of blood in the shooting, but the doctors decided not to give him transfusions because they were worried about the possibility of the AIDS virus in donated blood.)

LeMond's first serious training began after the Montana trip, when he started riding an hour and a half a day, working up to two hours a day after a week.

"I came back from nothing. I'd been training about three weeks, riding with a guy who kept dropping me all the time. I was becoming demoralized. Here I had won the Tour de France, and now I was being left behind by some guy riding back roads in California! Then one day I dropped *him*. I started feeling like a normal racer, an out-of-shape racer, but not one with a disability."

But as the French say, never two without three: the crash that broke his hand, the shooting—and then an appendectomy. "On July 16 we were around Santa Rosa when I had stomach pains. We checked into a hospital emergency room and they said it could be food poisoning, which is what I thought, too. We came home, but the next day the pains were worse, and I went to another emergency room. They thought it might be complications from my operation, so they opened me up to find out. My appendix looked bad and they took it out.

"I was in the hospital about four days, and it was a major operation, not the usual appendectomy, since they had to cut over my shooting scar from the belly button on down for about four or five inches. But the pain was hardly anything! It was a picnic in comparison to the accident; I could have walked out the next day. I felt so good that I really felt I could ride my bike the day I got out."

He couldn't, of course, and the 1987 season was virtually over for LeMond. But he was looking forward to 1988 and, as always, remained upbeat.

"A lot of good came out of the hunting accident. I'd been racing pretty intensely for seven years as a professional, feeling a lot of pressure to perform, and I'd started feeling it. It had become hard to keep my enthusiasm, and a lot of it had to do with my team. At the start of 1987 I'd had very little motivation to race for La Vie Claire because of the way Bernard Hinault and some teammates had treated me at the Tour and in the Coors. But though I wasn't eager to come back, I did it. Maybe I should have taken a break completely from cycling. You've got to work and do your job, but a lot of people are workaholics; I think you have to strike a happy medium.

"That vacation in Montana was really a joy. When I take a vacation in the winter, I worry about eating too much and getting fat. I feel I should run or do something active. Everybody thinks you race from February to October and then have the whole winter free. It isn't true. There's an underlying pressure to always be in shape because that's what it takes to stay on top."

In retrospect, LeMond was far too confident about the immediate future. He looked forward to 1988, never doubting that he could recover quickly. He would have been shocked to know that in the two years before his victory in the 1989 Tour, he would win only one race, and that one a minor exhibition in Belgium.

"The shooting gave me a break that left me enthusiastic about cycling again," he said in August 1987. "Even though I didn't win the Tour this year, I think I have what it takes to do it again. I believe I'm now reaching my peak and can prepare for the last years of my career in full force.

"I really believe that I can put two, three, or even four more Tours in my pocket if another Bernard Hinault doesn't come along. Even if a new Hinault does appear, I believe I'm capable of beating him. Does that sound too confident? I don't think so. After my accident I was out of condition, but that's just a matter of building myself back up. It's a plus when it's not a cycling-related accident because there's no psychological handicap. If you have an operation on, say, your knees, you never know when the problem is going to return, and that can affect the way you ride. For me there's none of that.

"I think I'd have won the Tour in 1987 if I were in the same condition as in 1986. Barring accidents—a bad fall or something like that—I think I'd have won. I'm very good in Tours because I have what it takes to win—great recuperation. I've rarely had a bad day in the Tour. In 1986 I always felt good."

Ron Kiefel, who has competed with LeMond for a decade,

confirms this. "It's natural talent," he said in analyzing LeMond. "Also he's very driven. He has all the physiological features that make up a real champion, but also an incredible ability to recover. As everybody else starts getting weaker, he stays at the same level. I think it's something you're born with. Sometimes when we were kids he'd have been skiing instead of training, and he'd show up out of shape for racing, but he always came around quickly, whereas other people had to lay a good foundation, and if they tried to recover too quickly, they'd nosedive the rest of the year.

"It's also his mental makeup. Ever since he was little, he could take pain. He always seemed to be able to last a little bit longer than anybody else."

LeMond cannot explain why he recuperates so well. "Maybe I utilize my energy better than other people do. I have a much better heart and lung capacity than most people. A lot of it, too, is conditioning. I may race a lot, but my performance is usually steady. That's how you know when riders are taking drugs or not training well: they perform in spurts, good one week, bad the next. Inconsistency is a sign that something's wrong.

"But one of the biggest misconceptions about professional cycling is that it has to have dope controls because so many riders use drugs. That's baloney. Sure, you hear rumors about Renault, that the reason some of their riders have tendinitis problems is because they're on drugs. Well, I never saw anything while I was with the team for four years. Hinault's tendinitis was understandable; he's raced forever and done a lot of Tours. When Fignon tested positive in a race in Belgium in 1987, he was the first rider for Renault—or Système U, as the team was called then—to be positive in my memory."

LeMond acknowledges that he is often asked how prevalent drug use is in cycling, a question that was raised again after Pedro Delgado, a Spaniard, won the 1988 Tour despite a finding that he had taken a masking agent for steroids. Delgado was allowed to keep his victory because the drug he took had not yet been banned by the professional bicycling federation, as it had been by the International Olympic Committee.

"Cycling is the sport most scrutinized, far more than any other," LeMond said, noting that in an average year he had at least thirty drug tests. "Baseball players say, 'I'll agree to do one drug test a year,' but we have to do it all the time." In the Tour de France, for example, the first two finishers each day, plus two riders selected at random and the rider in the yellow jersey at the start of the stage have to pass a urine test. "That's each day of the twenty-four days of the Tour. In 1987 two guys tested positive; in 1986 none did. But all the publicity makes the public think we're taking something."

LeMond gets agitated at the unfairness of the implication. "People are ignorant if they don't realize that there's as much or more use of drugs in marathon running or triathlons, sports where it would be beneficial to take something. Triathlons don't have drug tests, and the 1986 New York City Marathon was the first to have dope tests. In cycling, we've been doing it for twenty years. Football, basketball, and baseball players have admitted taking drugs just to feel good. Nobody suggests that *all* football players are on drugs, but a lot of people feel free to say that about my sport. Cycling has a bad rap on it, but I can honestly say that it's pretty clean.

"Of course a small minority of cyclists do use drugs. There are more than seven hundred professionals in Europe. A lot of them are broke, and they're all human. There are few people who, knowing that if they take something they may do better, are capable of refusing it. But the tests are pretty strict, so I honestly believe there is very little drug use in the major events.

"In smaller races where there are no drug tests it can be a different matter. Not everybody in those races is riding on water. I've ridden prologues—short time trials—in some of those races and guys I normally beat by forty seconds finish only ten seconds behind me, so I can tell something is going on.

"Sometimes, in races without dope tests scheduled, they spring surprise tests. You don't know about it until the race starts, or maybe you didn't even hear about it beforehand. Then your team car pulls alongside and tells you that they've pulled your number at random for a dope control. I've seen some races where guys' jaws drop when they hear the news. It's mainly the second-raters who do it."

LeMond is blunt in condemning drug users. "The guys who take dope are fools. Steroids can be really harmful. It's a dependency; if they take drugs and do well in one race, then they want them for the next race. They do one hundred twenty races a year, and they pay for it in the end by shortening their careers. Look at the longevity of a cyclist and you'll realize that he couldn't be taking many drugs. Overall, I believe the sport is as fair as it can be."

Further, LeMond points out, there is no alcohol abuse at all. "You simply can't drink when you're racing. Guys drink during the winter, and have enough beer to satisfy themselves. Not during the season, though. Alcohol is detrimental to exercise; there's no benefit from it. It reduces the force of the heart's contractions, so less blood is pumped through your body after you've been drinking. It increases the amount of oxygen your body needs, so you get tired quicker. Also, your muscles need more carbohydrates when you're drinking, so your body runs out of fuel quicker, and because it increases sweating, it makes you become dehydrated faster. Not much to recommend it to a bike racer, is there? Some riders may have a glass of wine with dinner, but that's the extent of it. It's a question of moderation, and most racers are good about that. Why shouldn't we be? We're talking about our livelihood.

"American cyclists used to be different. When I was growing up, we'd all go out and have four or five beers after we'd raced. You just can't do that as a professional; there's too much energy wasted, and every bit of it is needed to recuperate, especially in a stage race.

"That leaves only sex, and that's the biggest joke of them all. There are so many superstitions about sex in Europe. Sean Kelly claims that he doesn't make love for six weeks before the Tour. When I was with Cyrille Guimard you weren't allowed to have your wife around during the Tour, and if you got caught you'd be in trouble. I don't believe in those theories. I've had my best races and won the world championship after making love the night before. I don't say you should have sex immediately before a race, but the night before is something else again."

LeMond mocks most of the traditional thinking as nonsense. "So many people believe that if they don't take their vitamin pills in the morning, it's going to affect them psychologically and they won't race well. Or that if they make love the week before a race, they'll do badly. These riders have a psychological dependency. So much of it is built on the theory 'That's what the old racers did. Coppi, Merckx, they never made love before a race and that's the way I've got to do it.'

"Not me. I never grew up with those superstitions. I got into cycling when there was a big push in physiology, and a lot of attention was devoted to sex. Now researchers have learned that sex is the equivalent of walking fast up three flights of stairs. Three flights of stairs!

"Groupies? They're rare in cycling. French riders talk a lot about girlfriends, but it's mostly talk. You never see girls around a hotel during a race like the Tour de France. Impossible! When it comes to the Tour, everybody's serious. We're professionals, not sixteen-year-old athletes."

All the talk about sex, drugs, and alcohol brought LeMond

back to his recovery, and from there it was a short leap to his recuperative abilities while racing.

"There are times when I'm really exhausted in the Tour, but I know that everybody else is just as tired," he said. "That helps me mentally. Also I think I'm a pretty good bluffer, something you have to be to do well in long stage races. Sometimes you can't tell if you're going to have a good day, and then you have to bluff and pretend. The main point, I think, is not to change the way you do things every other day, so that nobody knows how you're feeling. If you're tired, you still try to race the same way and in the same position. That's hard at times; for example, Hinault always liked to ride at the front, but when he was having an off day he'd ride there only until the pack took off, leaving him behind. Then you knew he was bluffing.

"Riders bluff in different ways. A lot of them will act aggressive and attack when they're dead, but I like to ride consistently and keep people guessing. As a matter of fact, I never had to bluff when I won the Tour. There were a couple of days when I was extremely tired, but my body always responded quickly and I recuperated well. I'm still one of the youngest riders on the Tour and I feel I have the most potential. I'll bet any amount of money I'll succeed. My prime years are yet to come. Okay, so I broke my wrist, got shot, and had my appendix out. They say everything happens in threes. Everybody has one bad year. That was mine. Now it's over." They were brave words and, as it turned out, untrue.

11

Small Steps on the Way Back

Johan Lammerts, one of Greg LeMond's closest friends among professional bicyclists, was his teammate and roommate during the 1989 Tour de France. Reserved, even grave, the Dutchman was born only a year before LeMond but seems much older; in his protective and consoling way, he could be mistaken for an older brother of the American. He was in the hotel room when LeMond wept during the Giro d'Italia and talked about quitting the sport forever. Lammerts will confirm this, since LeMond has made it public, but offers no details. Exactly what Lammerts said to comfort LeMond remains their secret.

LITTLE BY LITTLE it was all coming back. First to return was Greg LeMond's natural optimism. Next came most of the weight he lost after he was shot, then his muscle tone. Last were his cycling legs.

"I'm not there yet, nowhere near, but slowly I'm getting

better," he said in the fall of 1987 just before the Créteil–Chaville race around the southern suburbs of Paris. "For somebody who didn't ride a race from March to September, I think I'm on track. This is all preparation for next year. All I'm trying to do now is finish each race I enter and add a few more miles to my legs. It will probably take me five or six months to increase my capabilities to where I was last year."

LeMond had to struggle through the Créteil–Chaville race. A man who never met a mountain he didn't like, he was left behind on the climb up the Madeleine Hill in the village of Chevreuse. In the Tour, the Madeleine would rank as a minor difficulty. "It took something out of me," LeMond admitted after he had showered and changed into casual clothes for the drive home to Belgium. "Still, I did the race and that's what counts, building my legs up. When you lay off, you lose a lot of muscle."

He had been more optimistic before the race while chatting with two teammates, Johan Lammerts and Steve Bauer.

"What do you hope for?" LeMond asked Bauer.

"Top five," Bauer replied.

"How about you, Johan?"

"Top three, maybe top one."

"Me, top twenty," LeMond announced. "That would be an accomplishment."

None of them fulfilled his expectations. Bauer finished 22nd, Lammerts 59th, and LeMond was not in the first sixty across the line. In that half hour of camaraderie before the start, LeMond took great comfort from his showing in the recent Tour of Ireland, where he had finished 44th. "I did better than half the field," he said. "A lot of people finished behind me."

Of the pace of his recovery, he remarked, "Saying I'm happy might be exaggerating, but it's fair to say I'm satisfied.

It was really hard to come back to Europe and begin racing early in September. Until then all I'd had was training rides. They're fine for training, but nothing makes you race-tough like racing." Between the shooting and his emergency appendectomy, his weight had dropped fifteen pounds, to one hundred forty, and he had lost nearly an inch off his thigh muscles. Now his weight was back to one hundred fifty pounds and he seemed fit.

Negotiations to quit the Toshiba team for PDM were moving ahead, he reported. "They act happy to have me. Quite a change from Toshiba. I think I'll get tremendous public support with PDM because the Dutch don't have anybody who's going to win the Tour. The Dutch have very good riders, but right now they're not capable of winning the Tour, and in that small a country national pride is a big factor."

A few months later, when he began the new season of 1988, LeMond continued to talk of winning the Tour, though he admitted that he was far from his best form. "It seemed I was fit last year because my legs were thin," he said, "but I had no power, no strength, I couldn't sprint, and I went into oxygen debt very quickly." The ability to reach oxygen debt late to delay the onset of pain as lactic acid builds up in muscles because of lack of oxygen in the blood—helps to separate champions from ordinary riders. Another demarcation is the ability to bear pain and keep pedaling. Suffering is what professional bicycling is all about, and champions suffer the longest.

The ability to suffer can be heightened through training, which is why racers go out on the road for up to seven hours most days during the winter and early spring. "Training is more an art than a science," explained Ron Kiefel. "You can't say, 'I ride six hundred kilometers a week and that guy rides

eight hundred kilometers a week, so he's in better shape.'
That's not the way it works. If a racer thinks he's doing things
right, he's on track." Alone, with a friend, or behind a motor
pacer, the average rider logs thousands of kilometers of training even before the season begins in February. Later, once the
spring classics—a half-dozen demanding and prestigious one-
day races—start, a rider continues to train most days of the
week, in sunshine and rain, until the major multi-day races
begin in late April and May. Some riders, LeMond among
them, also train indoors on stationary bicycles or vary their
training between short runs and long hauls to build up their
legs and cardiovascular system.

The previous November LeMond had been forced to drop
out of the modest Tour of Mexico when the mountains became too demanding. Then, in February, he'd started the
season with a feeble showing in a minor Spanish race, the Ruta
del Sol. "One day I had to be pushed up some of the hills,"
he admitted. According to some who had seen the race, the
truth was even worse: PDM teammates had to ride alongside
him, put a hand in the small of his back, and push LeMond
along even on the flat before he could finish a stage. In the
small world of professional bicycling—some eight hundred
riders spread over more than fifty teams, mainly in western
Europe—the word went out that LeMond was finished. He
heard the doubts and saw the smiles. But while making his
new beginning, he insisted that he never shared those doubts.
"Me?" he asked jokingly. "Me not sleep through the night
because I'm worrying? You've got to be kidding."

In March 1988 LeMond was lying on his bed in a shabby
hotel in the village of Fossacesia Marina on the Adriatic in
Italy, once again competing in the week-long Tirreno–
Adriatico race, the same one in which he had fallen a year
before, breaking a bone in his left hand. Putting aside a collection of short stories, he listened to questions.

The shooting was still vivid physically as well as mentally. Scratching his shoulder, LeMond said, "I can feel a pellet in my shoulder, but it won't come out for a while. Some of them will stay there—part of my body now, part of my character."

LeMond seemed more sure of himself than he had before his shooting. Such close friends as Kent Gordis, the television producer, agreed. "He's changed a lot since the accident. In the early stages of his fame I think he wasn't equipped to deal with all the demands. Now he's really matured and I'm extremely impressed. He seems more relaxed with himself. Maybe the shooting had something to do with it."

LeMond had something to celebrate that afternoon. He had come safely through the same stage of the Tirreno–Adriatico race in which he had broken his hand the year before in a mass spill that he had plowed into and gone down too. "Same hotel, same stage, same everything," he said, gesturing at the cheap room and its water-stained walls. "I've been careful since I started racing again to stay in the front or at the very back, nowhere in between. When I'm in good shape I avoid crashes because I'm strong enough to be in the front. Last year I was in the middle coming around a corner, and here were all these guys on the road. There was no way to hear them put on their brakes because the television helicopter flies so low in Italy that it drowns everything out."

There was something else to celebrate: LeMond had registered his first European victory since cruising up the Champs-Elysées a year and a half before as the winner of the Tour. This triumph was humbler, a sprint during the day's stage that awarded him three bonus seconds to be deducted from the overall accumulated time that decides a bicycle race. "I wasn't even going for it, but when it came down to the sprint I was in good position and I went for it."

LeMond is proud of his sprinting ability, and he talked about a rival, Sean Kelly, who usually rides well in the spring.

"He's the type who needs just a month of training and boom! he's right on top. That's why he does so well in Paris–Nice and the spring classics. He wipes the rest of us away in the spring. Maybe it's a question of body types. He's really a sprinter, with a much different body from mine. I have the build of an endurance rider, which needs a lot more work to attain a high level of fitness. Kelly can rarely drop me during a race, but the main difference between us is that he's a natural sprinter and I'm not.

"If I had a sprint like Kelly's, I'd rack up a ton of victories. But I just don't have it. Though there is a way to improve your sprint, the ability is hereditary; either you've got it at birth or you don't. Not that I have to apologize. I think I have one of the better sprints among endurance riders, but the truth is that except for bonus sprints in the Tour, I don't sprint. I don't take that chance and get involved in all the bumping that goes on in a typical sprint, including people pulling on your jersey to hold you back. Who wants to think about being knocked down or just plain falling with 150 guys coming up behind you like a runaway train? Those guys don't think before they sprint, they just do it. You win a lot more races that way. But I prefer to ride conservatively because I know my first obligation is to the Tour."

As in so many of his conversations, LeMond had concluded again with a mention of the Tour. His yearning to win it again had become an obsession, and he was unhappy that, to eliminate some long and predictably uneventful stretches, the race had been reduced by 1,000 kilometers from its previous length of more than 4,200 kilometers. "It's a joke that they've shortened the Tour; it's what cycling is all about," he said.

A shorter race would not help him, LeMond felt. "I prefer it the harder the better, the more mountains the better. When you have only one or two days in the mountains, everybody is fresher. Just when riders are ready to crack, they get an easy day. A lot of riders can endure one day in the mountains, and most of them can take two, but very few can handle three. It actually benefits the climbers when there are fewer mountain stages because pure climbers are much more fragile. They usually do well for one day, but to do it again and again is much more difficult. For the strong riders, the harder the race, the better we do."

Note the "we" when he mentioned strong riders. Yes, LeMond was feeling good. By winning the bonus sprint that afternoon, was he sending a message to his competitors? "I did that in the U.S.," he replied. After the fiasco of the Ruta del Sol, he had gone to Venezuela to race in the two-part Tour of the Americas. It was not an overly demanding race since the second part, through Florida, was flat, but he was pleased that he finished fourth in the U.S. stages and second overall in the race. "The change from Ruta del Sol was fifty percent." The first day in the Tour of the Americas there was a twenty-kilometer climb and he was afraid he'd be left behind, or "dropped," as riders say. "Some of the riders who had dropped me easily in the Ruta del Sol race were there, but this time it was me who dropped them. It was a good feeling because I knew I was on track again. When I start well in February it means I'm going to have a good season."

Confident but never cocky, LeMond was convinced at this moment that he was on the verge of a triumphant comeback. Life had been good since his move to Wayzata, near Minneapolis, which he described as his "favorite city now in the U.S. I love it." All winter he had worked to rebuild the power of his 5-foot-10-inch body, and all spring he rode the European circuit to regain his endurance. From Spain to France to Venezuela to Florida to Italy, then back to Spain, and on to Belgium and the Netherlands, he rode one-day and stage races and clocked thousands of kilometers in training rides. His goal was simply to stand again on the victory podium in Paris and be acclaimed as the winner of the world's premier bicycle race.

"I'm on track!" LeMond exclaimed joyously a few days later in the Italian resort of Porto Recanati as he sprawled on a massage table while a masseur kneaded his legs. "I don't think there'll be any problems," he went on. "I might even be good for the Giro," the Tour of Italy. "I'm hoping that by then I'll be well enough to win. All it takes is time and racing. I haven't forced myself at all. I think a lot of people who come back make that mistake: they try to do too much too soon. Power is the key factor. First you concentrate on that; then the cardio-vascular system will come around quickly, within a couple of months."

Before the shooting, LeMond admitted, he had been sick of the constant training. With the move to Minnesota, he felt he had found an alternative. In his new home on a small hill overlooking Lake Minnetonka, he had two stationary bicy-cling machines for indoor training, plus cross-country skis. "In cross-country you sort of skate with your skis, and it's very good for the legs and upper body. I'm a true believer now that I can do cross-country skiing, power training on my stationary bike, and weight training. After all that I need only an hour a day outdoors on the bike in the winter."

Another observer who had no doubt that LeMond would make it back to the top was his masseur, Otto Jácome. A major reason for his confidence was that LeMond's injury was not bicycle-related. "He didn't hurt his tendons, his knees are fine, the vital organs will heal themselves. Also he's clean; he's never taken any drugs. He won't even take vitamin shots. That will help him too." Jácome tapped his chest. "It's his cardiovascular system," he said. "It's a gift, you have to be born with it. He can start at zero with a bunch of riders, do exactly the same amount of training as they do, and in a race everybody else will be dropped but Greg will not. There's another thing: he's got wonderful talent and works at it, but he also has the ability to see things in a race that others don't. He looks around. The other riders are bent over their handlebars, concentrating, and they don't see. Nothing can surprise him."

Jácome, who has known LeMond since he was fifteen years old and who proudly says, "I predicted way back then that someday he'd be world champion," had been hired that winter by LeMond's new team, PDM. "I'm fitting in well with them," LeMond said. "They're easy to work with, and the riders are all friendly. They're also competitive, which is good. You want that; you want them all to have ambition. I'm the leader, but you want a team to ride for whoever's riding well, whether it's me or not. I don't want to be the leader for every race because to accomplish that the whole team has to be sacrificing for you, and when you come to the finish of Milan–San Remo, out of all the riders in contention you have to be absolutely certain that you can beat them all." At this point in his comeback, he did not yet have that conviction.

Besides the riders, PDM pleased LeMond with its philosophy. "It's a classy organization, calm, no pressure, but they get their message across. They know their riders are professionals and know how to do their job. Too many managers in cycling feel they have to tell you how to eat your dinner, when to go to bed, when to get up in the morning, and how to train. Maybe that's good for a nineteen-year-old who's just turned professional, but for somebody who knows what he has to do to perform well, it's worthless."

PDM, a Dutch joint venture between Philips and Du Pont

to make magnetic tapes, seemed equally happy with LeMond, whom it was paying a base salary of $350,000, with victory bonuses that might double the figure. "He's a classy boy," said Jan Gisbers, the team's manager, "and there are no language problems, even though most of the team is Dutch. When he's around, the other riders speak English. Of course it should be even easier in the second year of his contract. The first year a new rider doesn't know instinctively what the others will do in a race, so there's a lot of learning ahead."

The team was restrained about LeMond's chances in the coming Tour de France. "When you want to be the best team in cycling and to publicize the sponsor's name, you have to try to win the Tour," said Harrie Jansen, a PDM official. The team was then in its second year of existence and had an annual budget of 4 million Dutch guilders, about $2 million. For this investment, Jansen said, PDM expected to get seven times the money in publicity value. Before becoming a sponsor, the company had taken a poll of ways to achieve instant recognition, and believed that professional bicycling was quicker and cheaper than any other means.

Having LeMond in a PDM jersey would only help the cause. "We don't think he can win the big Tours this year, but we're hoping he can participate in the battle for the first three places," Jansen said. "Our investment in Greg has nothing to do with the American market; for the moment all our money is invested in Europe. We needed a star, but not a man of one nationality. The point about LeMond is that he is more or less above nationalities. He's not a Dutchman, an Englishman, or a Spaniard; he's interesting for every country."

A teammate's view came from Gerrie Knetemann, a thirty-seven-year-old veteran who was world professional road champion in 1978. "Greg makes a good impression—or at least not bad, and in these days not bad is already good." What

Knetemann meant was that since Bernard Hinault's retirement, the pack of riders had not had a dominating leader, a sure favorite in the Tour de France. In 1988 the race would be wide open, so why shouldn't LeMond be a contender?

In the spring, all things seem possible.

12

"Always Starting Over"

Professional bicycling has been defined as an individual sport practiced by teams. In one way this is basically true, for team ranking means almost nothing; the parts far outweigh their sum total. In addition to the individual winner of the Tour de France, say, there is a team winner computed on the overall standings of each team's finishers. But all the glory goes to the rider who won the Tour and none whatsoever to the top-ranked team, a distinction so small that nobody bothers to report it. What people remember is not that PDM is the top team in the sport but that for the last two years the Tour de France has been won by former PDM riders, Pedro Delgado in 1988 and Greg LeMond in 1989. PDM has everything, people say, except patience.

BARELY TWO WEEKS later, Greg LeMond was competing in a minor race in Belgium when he crashed. Trying to resume training too quickly, he developed tendinitis in his right shin.

Because of the pain he could not finish another race, and by mid-May he realized that he was running out of time to prepare for the Tour de France at the beginning of July.

"The whole thing depends on this stupid tendinitis—tendon, tendon, tendon," he said. "I hate to say 'tendinitis' because everybody automatically assumes it's drugs. It was just a crash."

LeMond was unclear about the accident. "It happened at fifty kilometers an hour, so anything could have hit me. I don't remember. One guy went down, taking others with him, and I was one of them. All I remember is doing a flip, rolling on the ground, doing another flip, and landing on my back. I slid about thirty meters and landed on my head and shoulder. Luckily I was wearing a hard-shell helmet."

At first LeMond thought he had broken his collarbone, but the X rays were negative. He had to remain off his bicycle, though, and there his troubles began. "I took two weeks off, and for every week you take off, it's nearly three weeks to get back to where you were." Those weeks away from his fitness level in the Tirreno–Adriatico race ("I was feeling pretty good there; I wasn't going great, but I think my progression would have been better than it is now") put him back roughly to the point in the Ruta del Sol race where he had needed his teammates to push him to the finish.

"The injury is about three inches above the ankle, and it's just like you got kicked in the shin playing soccer," LeMond explained. "Because I started riding hard on it too soon, it got irritated and then inflamed. When I ride, I aggravate the sheath of the tendon, the scar tissue aggravates it and causes inflammation, and the inflammation makes it sore. After two weeks off my bike, I was really ambitious and did four races in the first week. I didn't finish any of them because I'd lost my conditioning. Then I went to Italy, trained hard in the hills, and burned myself out. It's just one thing after another," he added in one of his rare admissions of weariness.

Was he despondent? "I'm not down," he said, "but I'm disappointed. It's taking a little bit longer than I thought. Maybe I had some unrealistic goals. I had some decent results, but I forgot that I started from less than zero last year, and it's impossible to go from there to the top of professional cycling in less than twelve months.

"But I like the fact that a lot of people don't think I'm going to come back. It just gives me more incentive to prove them wrong. I do well in pressure situations. People think, He's not going to do well when there's a lot of pressure. But I do better when that type of battle is going on. It makes me nervous, but for some reason I'm the type that never gives up even if I want to. There are a lot of riders out there who stop and say they can't do it anymore. I rarely feel that in races that are important to me.

"Of course there are races I make a point of not being concerned about. Psychologically you have to concentrate on certain goals. You're competing so much that if you took every race seriously, it would be difficult to concentrate when it came to the one you really want to win. I know that when I'm in top shape, there are very few people out there who can beat me. There is a confidence factor."

Throughout the latest problem, LeMond said, his team-mates and PDM officials had remained behind him. "They're really supportive. It's incredible how understanding they've been. I feel bad because they've been so nice that I'd really like to do something for them. I want to race well. They trust and believe in me, and they realize that maybe it's going to take a little bit longer than everybody had hoped. I have no doubt that I'm going to come back—it's just a matter of time—but I'd hoped that it would be in time for the Tour. I'm optimistic, but I'm also trying to be realistic. I don't know what's going to happen. I've been in similar situations where

I haven't been good in May, and three weeks later I've been fine."

Everything would depend on the Giro d'Italia, LeMond continued, which was only a few days away. "If I can get through the Tour of Italy, it should make some beneficial change in my condition. I'm finding that I don't recuperate as quickly as I used to. I don't have the stamina I had before, and it's going to take me a little longer than I thought. Once I get into this season, it's going to be a lot better. In '84 I started the Tour in very bad condition and still got third. This year, even if I'm only in the shape of '84—and I'd be disappointed with that—I feel I'll be capable of winning."

However, the tendinitis—or tendon problem, as LeMond insisted on calling it—was threatening to put his conditioning far behind that of 1984. "Who knows?" LeMond said. "Yesterday I trained and my tendon was bad, but this morning it feels a lot better. In order to get rid of it, I have to take injections, an anti-inflammatory shot, nothing that will hurt my tendon or my health. Some doctors might give a cortisone shot, but this is a nonsteroid shot, special for tendinitis." Steroids are banned in professional bicycling, of course.

How painful was it? "When I ride easy, not at all. But when I was in the Tour of Romandie, I could feel it getting worse each day. On Saturday I pushed myself pretty hard in the mountains, and on Sunday I could barely pedal." Finally he had been forced to drop out of the race.

No longer was LeMond talking of being able to win the Tour of Italy. As his slide downhill continued, it had become merely a training race for the Tour de France. As always, however, he remained hopeful.

"I believe that if I can get through the Tour of Italy and do some training in the mountains afterward, I can be in contention for one of the top five placings in the Tour de France. Maybe. Honestly, I really don't know. I've never been in this situation before. But if I don't do the Tour of Italy, I won't be in condition for the Tour de France."

Like the Tour de France, the Tour of Italy lasts three weeks, but is less difficult because the race is usually tailored for Italian riders and avoids the highest mountains. The Tour de France would be tougher, not only the last week in the Alps but also the first ten days, which are usually spent on the flat, where teams without climbers battle for the prizes and publicity they cannot hope to get once the mountains are reached. A decade ago, some stars would arrive for the start of the Tour in mediocre condition and spend the first ten days working their way back into shape, but those days are over. "The problem with cycling," LeMond said, "is that in the last five or six years it's become so competitive. We're racing at full bore in February, doing races that riders never used to do until April. When I was starting, it was hard in February, but not as tough as it is now. Some riders are piling up more and more kilometers in December and January because they know that the only time they can do well is February, March, and maybe April. If you go to Spain in February now, you've got to be in tiptop shape or you'll get blown away. And all the crashes! It used to be that at fifty kilometers an hour it would be single file. Now you have to do sixty kilometers an hour to be single file; at fifty you're all bunched up."

LeMond seemed troubled that his body had betrayed him. As he puts it, his body is a tool and he knows that tool the way a carpenter knows his favorite saw. Asked about his heart rate, he can sound like a cardiovascular surgeon. "Resting? In the morning, if I've been training hard, the rate is forty-one to forty-three, but when I'm doing a lot of endurance rides and am well rested, it's about thirty-seven or thirty-eight. It's gotten lower in the last five years, and that's usually an indication of a larger heart from exercise. It's able to pump more volume with less beats. You get that from endurance training. Too much interval riding makes the muscle smaller, so your performance can go down and your resting pulse comes up.

"Do you realize that your body actually becomes addicted to exercise? On days that I don't work out, I get headaches. I need to go out and ride at least thirty minutes or an hour, or else play golf. Otherwise I'm tense and in a bad mood. Nobody realizes how fragile an athlete is."

As it happened, LeMond was even more fragile than he'd feared. On July 12, 1988, when the Tour de France was in full swing, he was in a hospital in Minnesota, being operated on for his tendinitis. "The doctors opened it and cleared it out," he explained later. "The sheath around the tendon had scar tissue, and the tendon was not gliding through smoothly." The operation was relatively minor, and he wore a cast for only a week, cutting it off early. A physical therapist had contradicted the advice of his doctor to keep the cast on for two weeks.

Doctors had been giving LeMond contradictory advice all spring about his tendon problems, he complained, and he felt that the PDM doctor had been the least helpful of all. "We had bad medical advice until we went back to the U.S. and got it straightened out in about a week," Kathy LeMond said angrily. Trouble was brewing with the PDM team, even if LeMond refused to talk publicly about it. Once again he had entered a relationship with high hopes, and once again he was facing rejection and bitterness. Why was disillusionment apparently endemic to his dealings with his employers and such heroes as Hinault?

"Greg is like the American nature, very individual," Harrie Jansen, a PDM official, said a year later when LeMond had long since left the team. Jansen is a likeable and thoughtful man, quick to praise and slow to condemn. He was personally fond of LeMond, whom he usually calls "Gregory," though he did not admire him professionally. "Fitting him into the team wasn't always easy," Jansen said. "He was with PDM in the hardest year of his career. He was trying hard and not succeeding, so everything made him nervous."

Jansen's complaint was about what he perceived as LeMond's lack of dedication. "I still have a postcard from him that he wrote after I told him he was not a professional, that he was acting like an amateur, not training enough, not taking care of his body, not concentrating. He wrote me a card in which he said I was wrong and that he was going to show me." The Dutchman was sitting at an outdoor café a few weeks after LeMond had won the Tour de France again, this time in the uniform of the ADR team.

"It was a year ago that he sent that card, so he showed me," Jansen graciously conceded. Yet he defended his criticism. "We felt that his training was not concentrated. His whole career he has eaten hamburgers, not worrying about what he drank or how he rested. He has so much talent that he can live like ordinary people. He was too fat, and he was still eating his hamburgers, his pizzas, his beers, his everything."

But the trouble went even further, Jansen continued. "Everyone is impressed by Greg, and he influenced many of the other riders. That's not good for the team. We thought he should have done his job better and treated himself better. Probably his tendinitis was due to his forcing his training too hard. We did everything for his tendinitis. Everything! We got doctors, acupuncturists, but he was never happy with us."

As always, the truth probably lies somewhere between the versions told by two decent and honest men. At the end of 1989, LeMond admitted that his condition was much improved from the year before. "What really helped me climb was losing two or three kilos," he said, meaning four and a half to six and a half pounds. "I haven't been this skinny since my accident. I didn't race enough. I'd go two or three months and then something would happen and I'd be off the bike for two or three months. It went that way for two years. My weight now is one hundred forty-eight pounds, and it was one hundred forty-four at the end of the Tour. Last year I weighed one hundred fifty-four to one hundred fifty-six the whole year. Think about pulling three extra kilos up every hill!"

Jansen was also critical of the contract negotiations that lasted most of the fall of 1988 while LeMond decided whether to remain with PDM for the second season of his contract. "We're not accustomed to his way of discussing contracts with his father and his lawyers," Jansen said, reflecting the standard European view. "His people were only trying to obstruct things; they didn't really go for the goal. We had arguments all the time. It wasn't necessary. His lawyers and his father tried to get the last penny."

As the 1988 season wound down, however, LeMond had more than the last penny on his mind. Another unrewarding year was ending with another attempt to recover from surgery, and for the first time he was beginning to sound unsure of himself. "I'm feeling better but starting over again," he said mournfully at the Paris–Tours race in October. "I'm always starting over."

Because it is held in the fall, Paris–Tours is nicknamed "The Race of the Dead Leaves," and they covered the muddy parking lot where the riders were getting ready. A chill was in the morning air, and LeMond looked peaked and pale as he fiddled with his bicycle. In his absence from the Tour de France, his teammate Steven Rooks had finished second and won the jersey of the best climber. Another teammate, Gert-Jan Theunisse, had also ridden well and showed unexpected strength as a climber. In addition, PDM had just announced the signing of Raul Alcala, a third fine climber, whom it had lured from the 7-Eleven team.

Understanding that he was no longer the undisputed leader

of PDM, LeMond tried to sound unconcerned about any rivalry with Alcala, a Mexican who was not renowned for his dedication to training but whose potential was large. The big question was whether Alcala, Rooks, and Theunisse would be willing to put aside personal ambition and work for LeMond while he continued his comeback. Could Alcala help him? "I think so if I'm good," LeMond answered. "I can help him, too. If I'm in good condition next year, I don't think there will be a problem. I've raced long enough with Rooks and he's made a big improvement. I think that when I'm at my best I'm a better rider than most, but if he's better than me, or Alcala is, what purpose does it serve for me to get twentieth place in the Tour? I'd rather help the team. I don't want to take the position of not working for anybody but myself."

LeMond had talked with the Fagor team, which was based in France, about the possibility of moving, but thought that his best interests lay in staying with PDM. "PDM is definitely the team to be on if you want to win the Tour," he said. "If I'm good with them, I can win the Tour for sure, whereas if I'm good with another team, there's a chance that I might not."

Although a second victory in the Tour de France remained his primary goal, LeMond no longer seemed certain of the timing. In March he had talked about 1988, but now in October he was talking of a longer range. "Next year could be a question because I don't know if I'll be at a hundred percent again. It could take me a year or two." Voicing his doubts publicly, he appeared shaken to hear his own words. Then whistles started blowing for the start and immediately he brightened, broke into a smile, and pedaled off to another race, another chance, another beginning.

More than two months later, LeMond learned how new the next beginning would be.

For a man who went quietly to bed at nine-thirty P.M. on

New Year's Eve, Bob LeMond came close to starting 1989 with a splitting headache. It wasn't drink, but business. He had spent weeks waiting for the phone to ring so that he would learn which team his son would be riding for. Not until noon of the last day of the year did he discover that the team would be unsung ADR, based in Belgium and the object of Greg LeMond's scorn not a year before. "I had an attorney when I was thinking about switching from Tapie in 1986," he had said in a conversation about why he valued his father as a business agent, "and he was trying to convince me to go with the ADR team. ADR! It's one of the weakest teams around, and there's no way it could help me win a race, let alone the Tour. The attorney thought that's where my future was because all he was thinking about (in my opinion) was his ten percent if I signed a contract with them." (ADR are the initials of All Drive Renting, a car-rental company, but the team was so undistinguished at the time that in Flemish, one of Belgium's languages, the initials were said to stand for Al De Restjes, meaning The Good for Nothings.)

Despite LeMond's lack of respect, ADR was eager to sign him for 1989, so eager that it announced the deal before it was made. "I know they announced it weeks ago," Bob LeMond said from his home in Nevada, "but it wasn't true. Not only untrue, it almost didn't happen. Everybody was saying that Greg had signed with ADR, but we came within twelve hours of having to stay with PDM."

On January 1, LeMond would have been contractually bound to another year with the Dutch team. However, the December 31 mail gave LeMond's lawyer the final link in a business deal with so many wheels within wheels that it might have been designed by Bibendum, the Michelin man. The letter contained a guarantee from the bicycling team in Colorado sponsored by Coors Beer. In the new year, LeMond would ride for *both* ADR and Coors, which together would pay him a reported $150,000 more than his $350,000 contract with PDM. If the Coors deal had not been made, ADR alone would not have been able to offer enough to entice the rider. Although Coors liked the package, Bob LeMond said, nobody with authority to sign papers had been around during the holidays, so he had watched the clock move toward 1989 and waited for the phone to ring. "I just hope we've done the right thing," Bob LeMond said. "You never know."

In Minnesota, Greg LeMond was decidedly optimistic. "I'm happy," he said. "It's going to be better for me." He explained that a large part of his dissatisfaction with PDM had centered on a complex business deal involving bicycles being sold by Team LeMond, the business organization that he and his father operate in the United States. In effect, PDM management objected to his sponsorship of a bicycle other than the brand the team used. Also, LeMond said, there had been a dispute over his salary for 1989. Because of his lack of results, PDM had balked at giving him the raise to $600,000 called for in his contract.

At PDM headquarters in the Netherlands, the account was similar. "It was too much a question of sharing Greg," said Jansen. "He wanted all sorts of conditions to let him ride in the United States and satisfy different sponsors than our team has. His contract terms were simply unacceptable, especially the guaranteed raise after the bad year he had. We took a risk on him last year and we were willing to do so again, but it was impossible to agree to his conditions."

LeMond started the new year of 1989 characteristically upbeat. He conceded that ADR was not as good a team as PDM was, but brushed aside his new employer's lack of strong climbers to support him. "ADR has good strong workers. I'll be an isolated leader, but except for PDM most teams have isolated leaders. We have time to strengthen the team. Nobody says we have to do it all this year." His winter training was going well. "I feel strong, the fittest I've ever been at this time of year. I've done a lot of cross-country skiing, a lot of power training on my bike. I've taken only one week off all winter."

In less than two years LeMond had slid far downhill, going from number two in the computerized rankings of professional riders after winning the Tour de France to a humble number 345. He did not sound like a number 345 as he looked forward to the new year, bubbling with enthusiasm and hope. "With time, patience, and some luck, things may come my way again," he said. "I've just got to make it to the Tour of Italy without injury. If I do that and have some luck, watch for me in the Tour de France."

13

On the Verge of Quitting

Greg LeMond was sitting in a parked car before the final time trial in the Giro d'Italia, chatting with an American reporter, an old friend, and too polite to stop the questions just because he was due at the starting ramp in a minute or two. The reporter knew that LeMond had to set off at 14:47 but, as sometimes happens, he was confused about the twenty-four-hour clock that Europeans use and had it fixed in his head that LeMond was starting at 4:47. By now it was a quarter to three and even the ever-polite LeMond turned brusque. "Look, I've just got to go," he said, bolting from the car. "What's the rush?" thought the reporter, who then was stunned to see LeMond scramble up the steps to the ramp, carrying his bicycle and looking worried.

HE WAS FLYING down the road again, staying with the leaders, pedaling easily up the hills and skimming down in a strong, sure line on the descents. A pale sun lit the fields, where the first green shoots were pushing through dark loam. Spring is the time for hope, and once, just once, the next spring Greg LeMond genuinely felt that he had turned a corner.

After he finished sixth in the Tirreno–Adriatico race in March 1989, LeMond's hopes rose only a little, since he had also done well in that race the year before. But what seemed to be a big step forward came in the Criterium International, a three-day race in France that comprises a flat stage, a climb, and a time trial. All was normal on the flat stage until Stephen Roche and Laurent Bezault, team leaders for Fagor and Toshiba, jumped off in a breakaway. But it was not one of the usual breakaways that occur five or ten times in a race. The first men to go after them were Charly Mottet and LeMond, the leaders of RMO and ADR, who were quickly followed by Miguel Indurain and Laurent Fignon, the leaders of Reynolds and Super U, as well as Marc Madiot of Toshiba, and there began what the French call a "royal breakaway"—leaders directly accepting the challenge of leaders. The rule is simple: vanquish or be vanquished.

Fifty miles further on, at the finish, Madiot beat LeMond to the tape while the others rolled in just behind them. LeMond tried to play it down, but he was clearly happy that he had endured and recorded a strong second place. "The only reason I went with them was that I was at the front with them, and I was only there because I worry about crashing." His pleasure was obvious, however, and was not diminished by his sixteenth place in the time trial or his overall fourth place in the race.

Two months later, however, LeMond's hopes rang false. "Same old story: one step forward, two steps back," he said in May at the start of the Tour de Trump in Albany, New York. This should have been his shining hour, since he had long campaigned for a major American race with big prize money and top teams. "I like to race in the U.S. because I want to help cycling grow here. I see the future for me in this country."

Now, with $250,000 in prizes and such major European teams as PDM and Panasonic participating, LeMond had the fitting race—the one with such a puzzling name that Donald Trump was growing tired of all the jokes about it. Until then races had always traveled around the object of the preposition—thus the Tour de France, the Giro d'Italia and the Vuelta d'España. At no time, however, would the Tour de Trump, a ten-day, 837-mile race, circumnavigate Donald, the real-estate developer. Instead it would go from upstate New York to Manhattan, then pass through parts of Pennsylvania, Virginia, and Maryland before winding up on the boardwalk at Atlantic City, New Jersey. On the final day, the race would start and end at the Trump Plaza Hotel and Casino.

No matter about the name, Donald Trump said during a day replete with news conferences, television appearances, and autographing sessions. His sponsorship, he explained, had made the race successful even before the first wheel spun. "It's already turned out to be a tremendous success if you look at the coverage," he said, using the same yardstick that LeMond applies to European races. "Normally you'd have a bicycle race and nobody would be here."

Outside Trump's gunmetal-gray stretch limousine, a large, enthusiastic crowd stood in the Empire State Plaza, which looks like Brasília without palm trees, to watch the opening ceremonies. "I feel that when I attach my name to something, I have to make it successful," Trump continued. "My name is probably my greatest asset—and I have some nice assets." Or as he pointed out wryly at a press conference when asked why his race had not been called the Tour of America, "We could have done so if we'd wanted to have a less successful race."

The Tour de Trump got off to a fine start, attracting 114

riders on nineteen teams from twelve countries. Another sign of the race's importance was the seven and a half hours of television coverage it rated, including four hours by NBC, another sponsor. "We have the greatest teams and cyclists in the world," Trump summed up. "Some riders who didn't come are sorry now because they didn't have any idea how big this was going to be. It's never really happened in this country before. This race obviously means a lot."

With an option to promote the race for two more years, Trump was enthusiastic about its prospects. "It can go longer, it can go further," he said, blithely disregarding the necessary approval of the International Cycling Union. "Eventually we could have it begin in New York and end in San Francisco. Or we could go down to Philadelphia, Washington, and Baltimore; there are few places in the world that can top that in terms of population."

At times Trump had compared the Tour de Trump favorably to the Tour de France, but now, when questioned, he was more modest. "I have great respect for the Tour de France. To make the Tour de Trump as good as the Tour de France would be a tremendous honor."

The coming Tour de France would be the seventy-sixth, and the Tour de Trump had not yet logged a mile. Was it peculiarly American or peculiarly Trump-like to be comparing the two? With no hesitation Trump answered, "I think it's peculiar to me."

Why?

"Because I like to have big successes early."

In apartment buildings, gambling casinos, and yachts, in the private helicopter in which he traveled to and from Albany, Trump liked things big. "I have a tendency to overdo sometimes," he admitted. "We have a bigger production staff for this than is really necessary. I'd rather have a few extra security people than too few; I'd rather have too many cars than not enough. I think we've done it first class. I'd rather have it overdone than underdone, at least initially. I'm not guided totally by the dollar, despite what a lot of people think. I really operate more on the basis of what I think is good, what can work. That's one of the reasons I've become successful; I'm not necessarily guided just by the bottom line."

The Tour de Trump was a case in point. "It started as a fun event," Trump said, recalling the moment when the promoters who became his partners proposed the race. "When they suggested the name I wasn't even sure if they were serious. From there it just grew."

LeMond would have predicted this from the start. Professional bicycling may not have the appeal of baseball, basketball, or football for American fans, but presented as well as it was, this bicycle race drew big crowds almost everywhere.

The racers' arrival in a small town in Virginia was typical. Chris Lewis, Blake Nelson, and three other friends decided to cut high school in Sterling, Virginia, and run away with the Tour de Trump, the way kids used to do when the circus came to town. "Our mothers said it was okay," Lewis explained. "They wrote notes to school saying we were sick." Liberated, the sixteen-year-olds drove thirty miles south to Winchester and watched the race arrive to a joyous welcome. None of them bicycle fans before, the boys looked ecstatic as they gathered autographs from the riders.

Standing in the main street of the agricultural town of 23,000 residents, Sergeant R. A. Fox of the Winchester police seemed awed when asked to estimate the turnout. "About two thousand people waiting for hours in the rain," he said. "Not terrific by the Apple Blossom Festival standards, but pretty good for a bicycle race." Despite cool and rainy weather that had dogged the race from Albany to Allentown and Harrisburg, Pennsylvania, media coverage was intense and the crowds big and enthusiastic. The riders noticed it too. "You can't compare this with other American races," said Davis Phinney of the 7-Eleven team. "These are the kinds of crowds we get at European races. Maybe you have more people at the start and finish of a race in Europe, but we're getting the same turnout along the road, people lining up and cheering us on."

LeMond, who was riding for the Coors Light team rather than for ADR, agreed. "It's a much more European race than any that have been held here before," he said. "It must be the best organized race ever for its first year of existence, and the crowds have been super."

The $250,000 in prize money, among the highest in international racing, helped keep the riders enthusiastic. "That's a lot of prize money, which gets the racers excited," said Andy Hampsten of 7-Eleven. "The name Tour de Trump didn't mean anything to European racers, but when they heard that there was a quarter of a million dollars in prizes, they said, 'Let's go.' Also the organizers have done a very good publicity job."

Among the European riders there was surprise at how difficult the race was. Steven Rooks, second in the 1988 Tour de France and a consistent high finisher in the spring classics, was one of these. Asked early in the going if the foreigners were along just for a vacation, he denied the charge, but privately he changed his story a few days later. "I came for a holiday," he joked, "but this isn't one at all. Next time for a holiday I'll go somewhere with a beach."

Television coverage helped to keep the publicity flowing. "It can make or break a sport," said Jim Ochowicz, the general manager of 7-Eleven. "It's not only in the States; it's beginning to be that way in Europe, too. At some big races in Belgium there really aren't many spectators, but if it's on TV it stays big."

Still, NBC's first two-hour live program was disappointing in terms of viewers, with an audience share of about 1.7

points, considerably under the 3-plus average that CBS had attracted for its Tour de France coverage in 1988. "It's an educational effort," an NBC official said. "We hope to do better on the last day."

In fact, while the ratings were better, NBC bungled the coverage of the final time trial, choosing to center on Phinney, the American who was a favorite in the race against the clock, instead of either the race's overall leader, Dag Otto Lauritzen, a Norwegian, or his closest opponent, Eric Vanderaerden, a Belgian who was fifty seconds behind. By keeping its cameras on the American, who had only a middling result, the network failed to show Vanderaerden taking a wrong turn and riding three hundred or four hundred yards off the course before recovering. The lost time and the psychological blow left him nearly two minutes behind Lauritzen, who collected the winner's check of $50,000.

Unnoticed in all the uproar, Ron Kiefel of 7-Eleven won the time trial while using the innovative handlebars that triathletes favor to keep them in a strict aerodynamic tuck. The handlebars, usually called Scott bars, extend out from the standard handlebars and force the rider forward and down. They had not been used in a major professional race before the Tour de Trump, and surely would have attracted more attention if Vanderaerden had not strayed off course and then broken down in tears at the finish.

Where was LeMond in all of this? Nowhere, finishing an undistinguished 27th overall in the race that he had awaited for years. Worse, he realized that he was attracting little attention as reporters flocked to interview the riders with impressive results. The message was unmistakable: he was yesterday's story. The Tour de France victory three years before had put him on the first page of many U.S. newspapers, and the shooting had done so again, but now he was unable to make even the sports pages. "The Tour de Trump was the low point of my season, maybe of my career," he said later. "After the second day I wanted to stop. Afterwards I thought about having my lungs examined to see if there were some undiscovered pellets in there."

Worse was to come in the Giro d'Italia in mid-June. "I wanted to stop in it too," LeMond said. "I was planning to stop cycling altogether. I couldn't, but it entered my mind: Maybe I *am* finished, maybe there's something wrong with me. I had no strength at all in the Tour of Italy, even on the first climb." He lost eight minutes that day on what was not considered a difficult ascent of Mount Etna.

Kathy LeMond spoke about her husband's deepening gloom. "He was very depressed. He couldn't believe he'd been dropped by eight minutes in the first climb. It had never happened to him before, dropping to the back of the pack, riding with people who finish forty minutes down."

LeMond's ADR teammates began criticizing him, even mocking him and his condition. LeMond prefers not to discuss this. "Contrary to what a lot of people thought, I *was* dedicated," is all he will say. "I trained hard and put in a lot of effort last winter."

LeMond was down and nearly out. Then, in one of those wonderful moments that generally occur only in the movies, he learned that his problem was a simple physical one. "Otto noticed at the beginning of the Tour of Italy that my face was gray," he said, referring to Jácome, his masseur. "It was that way in the Tour de Trump too." Ever the sports fan, LeMond remembered that a running magazine had recently published an article about lack of iron in the blood. Iron is a binding product for oxygen and red blood cells, which supply oxygen to muscles throughout the body. "The article said the only vitamin that really makes a difference in performance is iron."

LeMond had been taking iron tablets for two months, and

they had not made a difference, but many people cannot absorb the mineral except through injections, he learned. Even after an analysis of his blood showed that he was extremely low in iron, he was unsure if this was indeed his problem. "I thought maybe I was just riding poorly." But after another dismal climbing stage at Tre Cime di Lavaredo, midway through the Giro d'Italia, he decided that there was nothing to lose. "It wasn't normal; I wasn't even putting out an effort. I couldn't take oxygen. So we did three iron injections, but even after the first one I started feeling much better. From that point on, I could feel I was improving and getting oxygen. The day before the last time trial was the first day I felt capable of staying with decent riders in the climbs. I was finally getting power. I hadn't felt that good for two years."

Welcome back, Greg LeMond. "Today or never in this Giro," he said while sitting in a car in the town of Prato, awaiting his start in the time trial that ended the 3,655-kilometer (2,263-mile) race in Florence. "I'm in a tunnel where I can't see the end," he continued, still refusing to believe that the iron injections would make a permanent improvement. "I'm doing better, but I'm a long way from being at my best."

As fans reached through the car's window for autographs, LeMond complied but kept talking gloomily, though never with self-pity. "Part of my problem now is that I have no knowledge of what my body will do," he said. "I have the experience, but my body . . ." His voice trailed off.

His comeback had also been slowed by other than physical troubles, LeMond acknowledged. "Sometimes it's mental. When I have a bad day, I have no hope or motivation. When I was young, I was always striving to get to a point, and I never thought twice about it. 'So I had a bad day,' I'd say to myself; 'tomorrow I'll have a good day.' Now it's 'I had a bad day; am I ever going to come back?' That's always the question."

With only the time trial of the Giro remaining, LeMond

ranked 47th, more than fifty-five minutes behind in the field of 141 riders. He needed a boost, he said, something for his morale, something to be hopeful about in the three weeks before the Tour de France. Perhaps this long time trial would be it. "I want to test myself today," he said cautiously. "I don't think I can win, but I want a good placing. It would mean a great deal to me."

Moving with the force that marked his best years, LeMond then went out and rode a dominating time trial. Within six kilometers he had caught the rider who had started a minute and a half before him. In fifteen more kilometers, he overtook and passed the rider who had left three minutes earlier. His back bent into his work, his line around curves tight and efficient, he pedaled past Tuscan villages and fields, down the right bank of the Arno River in Florence, past the Ponte Vecchio and thousands of cheering fans, across the river and up to the line that marked the finish. He did not quite manage to surpass the previous fastest time, 1.5:34, which had been set by Lech Piasecki, a time-trial specialist, but his clocking of sixty-three seconds slower was good enough for second place by more than a minute. All smiles, he coasted off with the memory of at least one more good day. "The Giro time trial," he said months afterward, "was the race that turned things around. It gave me a lot more confidence."

LeMond was not the only one to turn a corner that day. The overall winner of the Giro was Laurent Fignon, who also was emerging from the shadows. After his victories in the 1983 and 1984 Tours de France, he went into a steep decline as he tried to overcome a year's layoff became of surgery for heel tendinitis. Each year he seemed on the verge of a comeback, winning the Milan–San Remo classic twice running, for example, and each year he fizzled in the Tour. Indeed, since the surgery he had finished the Tour only once, and in 1988 he had cracked long before the mountains and quit during the first day in the Alps.

Each failure left a scar and Fignon began to believe that he could no longer climb or do time trials, two of his previous strengths. As he prepared for the final race against the clock in the Giro, he was thinking how he had lost the 1984 race. He had finished second then to Francesco Moser, an Italian hero, and many observers felt that he would have won if the race's organizers had not canceled a mountain stage in which Moser, a notoriously poor climber, probably would have lost his lead. The official explanation for the cancellation was that a fresh snowfall had blocked the pass over which the day's stage was to run, but reporters who drove there found it open and nearly free of snow. Moser used the respite and the new aerodynamic disc, or covered, wheel to stay barely ahead of the Frenchman in the final time trial.

But this time Fignon was in fine form and finished fifth in the time trial, bearing down to clock the fastest time over the last kilometer. His victory was unpopular in Italy, and not merely because the runner-up was Flavio Giupponi, a hitherto obscure Italian. In the final eight days of the race, after earning *la maglia rosa*, the pink jersey of the leader, the Frenchman had exuded a confidence that many Italians regarded as arrogant, even contemptuous. Leading Giupponi by only seventy-six seconds and Andy Hampsten by eighty-nine seconds with three stages to go, Fignon won a sprint finish and came back the next day on a tiring mountain stage to finish third, just ahead of Giupponi and Hampsten. "Fignon went out of his way to let everybody know how well he's going," said Lauritzen, the Tour de Trump winner, and as the crowd filed away from the final line in the Piazzale Michelangelo, under the magisterial glare of a copy of Michelangelo's statue of David, the Frenchman did indeed seem confident about his prospects in the coming Tour de France.

"He's back, no question about that," said his team manager, Cyrille Guimard. "He's very good right now," agreed Le-Mond, once Fignon's teammate and rival and now simply his rival. "*Very* good, maybe as strong as in 1984."

The Tour de France was three weeks away.

14

"So Far, So Good"

*Later, of course, people would write that Greg LeMond should
have ranked among the favorites in the 1989 Tour de France.
His form had been coming around, they would say, citing the time
trial in the Giro. The Tour was wide open, they would claim,
with no dominating rider present, no Bernard Hinault or Eddy
Merckx. Afterward it would all seem so clear, but two months
earlier, in Charlottesville, Virginia, during the Tour de Trump,
Greg and Kathy LeMond had laughingly related how much easier
their life was these days; the telephone never rang with reporters'
questions, fans had stopped coming to their door, nobody seemed to
have any interest in Greg. They seemed both relieved and saddened
by this.*

ONLY THE STUDENT PRINCE was missing as Luxembourg wel-
comed the Tour de France. From cafés serving beer in rococo
steins to the guardsmen pacing at the Grand Ducal Palace, the

operettalike air of the capital was astir with autograph seekers, photographers, and just plain gawkers. Even the routine medical examinations that the 198 riders had to take for the race were thronged with spectators. Of the twenty-two teams of nine men each, five came from France; four each from the Netherlands, Belgium, and Spain; two from Italy; and one each from Switzerland, Colombia, and the United States. The riders were competing for a jackpot totaling 8 million French francs, about $1.2 million, easily the biggest purse in cycling.

At the center of attention was Pedro Delgado, the Spaniard who had won the year before. "That naturally makes him the favorite this time," said Bernard Hinault, now an official with the race. "Also he's been riding very well, has trained hard, and is extremely motivated." Hinault was alluding to the scandal that had ensued the previous year when Delgado was found to have used a masking agent for steroids. The drug had been banned by the International Olympic Committee, but not yet in professional bicycling, where the authorities acted against it only a month after Delgado won the Tour. In effect the Spaniard had slipped through a loophole to keep his yellow jersey.

Eddy Merckx, who like Hinault had won the Tour five times, also alluded to the scandal when he named Andy Hampsten, his protégé, as his choice. "Delgado should be, but . . ." Merckx said. Asked to clarify, the Belgian gestured to imitate a man with the weight of the world on his shoulders.

Hinault and Merckx were not alone in remembering Delgado's torment in the final week of the 1988 Tour. The Spaniard recalled it too. "The fans were very kind to me last year, but there are still some bitter memories," he said. "I know I have something to prove, and I hope to do so."

Delgado seemed genuinely pleased by the topographic outline of the 2,025-mile (3,250-kilometer) race. The Tour de France, which has been stopped only by world wars since it began in 1903, presented a heavily mountainous profile as its seventy-sixth edition prepared to move counterclockwise around the mother country. Two days were to be spent in the Pyrenees and four days in the Alps, one more than the previous year. Besides a short prologue, or individual time trial, on the first day and a team time trial on the second day, three individual races against the clock were scheduled. The last of these would start in Versailles and end fifteen miles later on the Champs-Elysées on the final day of the race.

"It will be a tough race throughout," said Peter Post, the coach of the Panasonic team. "That extra day in the Alps!" exclaimed Hampsten. "It will be tense at the end—shorter, intense climbing." Asked who his favorites were, the American laughed. "My list this year is longer than ever." He ticked off Delgado, Laurent Fignon, Stephen Roche, and Steven Rooks, the Dutchman who had been second to Delgado in 1988.

The defending champion sounded confident. "Maybe the mountain stages are a little too short, but it looks good for me," he said. In words that became richly ironic a few days later, he added, "We'll ride very hard from the start, and I'm ready." After winning the Vuelta d'España earlier in the year, Delgado had spent more than two weeks alone in the mountains, training for the Tour de France. Despite his best efforts, controversy had a way of following him. He had been publicly rebuked during the Tour of Switzerland a month earlier when the organizer accused him of not trying to win, but using the race only to prepare for the Tour de France. More seriously, after his victory in the Vuelta he was accused of having paid a Russian rider to help him. Delgado's Reynolds team said it had investigated reports that he had been seen passing this opponent an envelope, and insisted that the Spaniard was simply giving the man directions for a visit to his home in Segovia.

"All that is over now," Delgado said. "I am very happy to be here in Luxembourg."

Why Luxembourg? Every few years the Tour de France begins abroad in such places as Frankfurt, Basel, Berlin, or Leiden. The incentive is money. Little Luxembourg, with a population of 372,000, had reason to pay about $1.5 million to have the race spend two full days and part of another in the 999-square-mile country.

"In a sense this is the cradle of modern Europe," said Gaston Seil, a spokesman for the local organizers. He referred to the 1950s treaties that established the European Coal and Steel Community, the European Economic Community, and the European Atomic Energy Community, whose bureaucracies are based in Luxembourg.

In addition, 1989 marked the 150th anniversary of the Treaty of London, in which France, Prussia, and Britain renounced designs on Luxembourg's green, mostly empty territory. "So there is a reason to celebrate," Seil said. "But mostly we wanted to have the best riders here and see them in person, not on television."

Which, as it turned out, was nearly the only way the people of Luxembourg were able to see Delgado.

The race began in turmoil on July 1. Pushing his bicycle ahead of him and looking frantic, Delgado arrived at the starting platform two minutes and forty seconds behind schedule for the 7.8-kilometer (just under five-mile) prologue. Quickly he scrambled up the few steps to the platform, and just as quickly mounted the bicycle and pushed off with none of the ceremony usually reserved for the previous year's winner. Wobbling as he attempted to gain speed over the first few yards, the Spaniard pushed determinedly on the pedals and moved out of the sight of stunned officials. The lateness counted against him, and he finished the day last in the pack. As wags said, never before had a rider gone in one day from the yellow jersey of the leader to the *lanterne rouge*, or the symbolic red lantern that signifies the last man in the race.

Nobody could recall a previous leader who had shown up late for the start of any daily stage. "Once in a while a low-ranking rider will be late, but never the man in the yellow jersey," one official said. At the finish of the prologue Delgado said that he had simply lost track of the time. "I thought I still had a couple of minutes," he explained. Displaying no sign of his reputation as a worrier, he appeared calm, even joking, and he remarked, "It's not so bad. There are still twenty-one days left."

Some Spanish journalists disputed Delgado's version of what had gone wrong. They insisted that he had taken a wrong turn when he completed his warm-up near the platform in the center of the city. According to this account, Delgado had bicycled almost a block away from the start, moving through a thick crowd, before a team mechanic caught up with him. He finished the prologue in 12.48:30, including the 2:40 penalty, which left him more than a minute and a half behind the next-to-last man in the pack, Philip Van Vooren of LeMond's ADR team.

Lost in all the commotion was the surprisingly strong showing of LeMond, who finished fourth in the prologue, not usually a discipline he excels in. "I feel pretty happy with that," he said. "But it doesn't necessarily mean much. I have to be careful not to get confident too quickly."

"So far, so good," was the way LeMond summed it up twenty-four hours later, after the first two days' racing. The team time trial had gone better than most observers expected for ADR, which lost 55 seconds to Fignon's Super U team, while Delgado had slipped even further back. Changing out of his sweat-soaked racing uniform, LeMond was trying hard not to give in to optimism but to remain realistic, as he put it.

"It's been slow, so slow," he said again of his comeback. He brushed off the fact that he had just celebrated his twenty-eighth birthday. "I'm not getting old. That's not the problem; it's that I'm starting a new career. Do you know how hard that is?" For him it had been exceedingly hard, and he had scaled down his ambitions. Asked about his goals in the Tour, he said simply, "To do as well as I can.

"To do as well as I can," he repeated, "but I don't know what place that means." He thought about it for a moment, looking anguished. "My goal would be the top fifteen," he finally decided. "I'm setting some realistic goals. Of course I'd like to be in the top five, top three, but I have to be realistic. If I'm even in the top twenty it will be a successful Tour for me. And I'd really like to win a stage, especially a time trial."

Everything depended on his form, LeMond continued, and that remained uncertain. "I don't have the confidence I had earlier, because I had so many bad days in the Tour of Italy. In a couple of days there I lost so much time that I rode the rest of the race with no motivation. I have to guard against that here."

After Luxembourg the race moved through Belgium and into France, heading for its first big shakeout, the fifth stage and a 73-kilometer time trial from Dinard to Rennes in Brittany. Sportswriters often refer to a time trial as "the race of truth" because riders have no recourse to tactics or team support and can rely only on themselves. It is purely a test of strength and endurance, the ability to suffer while maintaining a steady speed. Concentration is everything, using tunnel vision to focus on the next twenty or thirty meters of a course that varies from twenty-five to seventy-five kilometers. No relaxation is possible in a time trial, no coasting around a curve or down a hill, no yielding to the need to shift one's body or to sit up straight awhile because the shoulders and lower back are knotted with pain from maintaining an aerodynamic tuck.

Cooperation is banned: each man rides for and by himself, and if he catches the man who left a minute or two ahead of him, he is not allowed to move into position behind his opponent's back wheel, gliding in the slipstream—or drafting, as it is called—and thus conserving up to 25 percent of the energy he would usually expend. Nor can a rider ask the team car following him for any assistance other than shouted encouragement and information about his time at key points. He may change bicycles or wheels, snatching a substitute from the team car, but he cannot receive any other mechanical help. The only assistance allowed the time trialist is in his equipment. To reduce wind resistance, aerodynamic helmets and special skintight jerseys are permitted, as are lightweight bicycles and disc wheels.

The morning of the Dinard–Rennes time trial, another piece of equipment was approved, one that would be of vital significance at the end of the Tour. The 7-Eleven team unveiled for officials the same triathlon handlebars that Ron Kiefel had used to win the final stage of the Tour de Trump back in May. Bringing along the venerated Eddy Merckx, now their official bicycle supplier, for reinforcement, the 7-Eleven officials pointed out that the Scott bars had been authorized for use by the American team in the 100-kilometer time trial at the 1988 Olympic Games in Seoul.

"Merckx made the difference," said a man who was present at the meeting. Back in 1984 when Francesco Moser had broken the Belgian's record for the hour's race against the clock by using disc wheels for the first time, Merckx had protested bitterly, railing that Moser's advanced technology disqualified him from holding the record without at least an asterisk attached. Hence, if he was supporting a new piece of equipment now, the International Cycling Union, the authorities who decide such issues, had to be impressed. "The judges thought that if Merckx said that the bars were within the rules, they must be," said the witness.

The 7-Eleven team was not alone in planning to use the innovative handlebars, which formed a long U extending from the standard handlebars and forced the rider forward and down. LeMond had not benefited much from the Tour de Trump in terms of glory or respect, but he too had noticed the success of the bars. They were invented by Boone Lennon, who sought to put cyclists in time trials into the same tight tuck that ski racers use, emphasizing a flat torso position and using padded supports to perch the rider's arms in front of his face. This hand position keeps the air flowing around the rider instead of piling up in the pocket formed by open arms. Some tests in a wind tunnel between the classic time-trial crouch and the praying-mantis position with the triathlon bars showed that the new extension could add up to two minutes over a twenty-five-mile course, though European racing officials insisted that their own tests proved nothing of the sort. Weighing the alternatives, LeMond decided to try the handlebars, and even invited Lennon to come to the Tour de France as a personal consultant who would set up his bicycle for time trials.

Before the race, LeMond was nervous, which he felt was a good sign, remembering his anxiety the morning before winning the world championship in 1983. The last few days had been going well, and he ranked fourteenth overall. "I've felt good ever since the prologue," he said, noting that even the little things were working out. Two days earlier, when the stage had ended in Wasquehal, near the border with Belgium, he had driven home, seen his family, and eaten a Mexican dinner cooked by Kathy. No racing was scheduled the following day because the riders were to take planes to Brittany for the time trial the day after.

But for once in the Tour de France pocket kingdom, which travels with its own police force, bank, and post office, something went badly wrong and one of the two chartered planes failed to arrive in Lille for the flight to Brittany. Half the Tour flew off in a Super Caravelle while the remaining teams drew lots to see who would board a smaller Fokker and who would have to wait for another hastily chartered plane. Luckily ADR came up a winner, so late in the afternoon, four or five hours later than scheduled, LeMond was finally able to cycle over the next day's course in Brittany. Such an inspection is important, because knowing where the major curves are and being able to cut them closely can reduce a long course by nearly a kilometer.

While LeMond and his close friend and teammate, Johan Lammerts, were riding the course, they met Roger Legeay, the coach of the French-based Z team. It was a fateful meeting, but as in most moments that change a person's life, who knew it then? All it seemed to be was a chance encounter between a struggling rider and a frustrated coach.

Legeay is forty years old and came up through the ranks; he had spent a decade as a rider with no great success. "As a racer I didn't have much class," he admits, "but I always worked hard." He was in seven Tours as a support rider before retiring in 1983 to become assistant coach of the Peugeot team. Three years later he was made head coach—*directeur sportif*— just as the team's primary sponsor, Peugeot Bicycles, withdrew from the sport. By then the annual budget was $2 million, and the sponsor could no longer afford it. So ended a long strain of cycling history; Peugeot had begun sponsoring riders in the 1890s, and for decades equipped and supported a large network of amateur clubs throughout France, drawing many riders for its professional squad from this farm system. Peugeot was known as a solid team and was often a winner; a decade earlier Bernard Thévenet had captured two Tours while wearing its conservative white jersey with a discreet black-and-white checkerboard. "We were the team kids dreamed about joining," said Gilbert Duclos-Lassalle, a Frenchman who began riding for Peugeot in the late 1970s.

What Duclos-Lassalle meant was French kids, which was precisely Peugeot's flaw; it was too *much* a French team. In 1968 it had refused to sign young Eddy Merckx when he insisted that three other Belgians be hired as teammates. In 1983 it alienated two fine English-speaking riders, Phil Anderson of Australia and Stephen Roche of Ireland, by favoring its French riders. In 1985 it failed to protect Robert Millar, a Scot, in the Vuelta d'España, allowing a Spanish cabal to snatch away his victory on the race's next-to-last day. Roche, Anderson, and Millar all left Peugeot to lead other teams. "It's tough to be a foreigner with Peugeot, very tough," said Dag Otto Lauritzen, a Norwegian, before he left it to join 7-Eleven.

When Legeay was told during the 1986 Tour that Peugeot was withdrawing its support, he started looking for another sponsor. He found Roger Zannier, a French manufacturer of inexpensive clothes for children, who was seeking publicity as he began to franchise stores under the label of Z—or Zed, as the French say. Quickly sold on the idea, Zannier showed that a new boss was in charge by introducing his own jersey. Out went the black-and-white checkerboard; in came a comic-strip motif shading from baby blue to navy blue while framing a big Z. Everybody agreed that you either loved or hated this design, especially the pink Z emitting what seemed to be a white exhaust puff atop a yellow starburst.

Zannier seemed realistic about providing the $2 million, or 10 million francs, necessary to keep the team going. "If I spend ten million francs for a team that's just one more in the pack, it's far too expensive," he said, "but if I spend twenty million on a team that can win the Tour, it's not expensive at all. I've given them three years to show me a Tour winner wearing my colors."

By 1989, the end of those three years, no rider on Zannier's team had come closer than seventh place to winning the Tour, and he was hinting that he might withdraw his financial support. Legeay was seeking solutions even as he led his team into battle. The afternoon before the time trial he had intended to drive the course behind his riders, but was delayed by a television interview, so he was alone in his car. "I saw LeMond and Lammerts returning from their inspection and decided to stop," he said months later. "We talked about one thing and another. Then I said to Greg, 'What are you planning to do next season? If you're free, I'd be interested.' "

In another sport this might be called tampering, but in professional bicycling it passes for polite conversation. Riders change teams often, and savvy coaches are on the lookout for somebody with a reputation like LeMond's, even if his recent results have been poor. Though LeMond had another year on his contract with ADR, he was increasingly unhappy with the team, and he filed away the question. At that moment there were more important matters on his mind, and first among them was the time trial that would define his standing in the Tour. For once the sportswriters' cliché was apt: LeMond was facing a race of truth.

15

Back in the Yellow Jersey

*The yellow jersey was first awarded in 1919, sixteen years after
the first Tour de France, because fans kept complaining that they
could not instantly identify the leader of the race. Henri
Desgrange, the founder of the Tour, chose yellow because it
matched the color of the pages of the newspaper he edited, L'Auto.
There are many Tours—even such tiny countries as Belgium, the
Netherlands, and Luxembourg stage their own, although they
usually last for three days, not three weeks—and many jerseys for
their leaders, but none approaches the prestige of the yellow jersey
of the Tour de France. Nobody ever seems to pull one over his
shoulders without a beatific smile.*

NOT FOR YEARS had Greg LeMond been so thrilled to stand
in the rain and receive a modest bunch of flowers wrapped in
cellophane. "It was like winning the world championship. It
was my best moment in many years," he said in exultation, still

clutching the ritual bouquet that stage winners receive. "I'm happier than when I won the Tour in 1986. This is the most wonderful day of my life. It's almost a miracle."

LeMond was speaking late in the afternoon of the time trial, after riding, in a rainstorm, twenty-four seconds faster than anybody else. Now he waited until the thirteen riders who had started after him reached the finish line before he mounted the few steps to the podium and accepted, for the first time since late July three years earlier, the yellow jersey of the leader of the Tour. "You can't imagine what I've gone through the last few years," he told interviewers. First among the people he wanted to thank was Kathy. "My wife has helped me so much that I want to dedicate this success to her." He had prayed for victory, he continued, and perhaps this had helped.

To another interviewer, LeMond confided a secret. "It's the bars," he told John Wilcockson, the editor of *VeloNews*. During his long warm-up for the time trial, he had tested the Scott handlebars by riding with a teammate, Janusz Kuum, who was using traditional handlebars. Watched by the ADR team coach, José De Cauwer, the two riders hit high speed before LeMond left Kuum far behind. "It's a simple question of aerodynamics," explained De Cauwer. "The air flows around LeMond, who with the handlebars is shaped like an egg, but it hits Kuum in the chest and slows him down as if his body was a parachute."

Despite the announced approval of international officials, none of the European riders used the handlebars at Rennes, or later in the two remaining time trials. Among the Tour teams, both PDM and Panasonic had sent riders, officials, and mechanics to the Tour de Trump, where Ron Kiefel had introduced the handlebars professionally, yet they still were given little credit for increasing speed. Boone Lennon, their inventor, had offered them to PDM and Panasonic, and had urged riders on both teams to try them. He had no takers among the Europeans. To the doubters, the evidence remained inconclusive. In the Rennes time trial, four 7-Eleven riders used them with varying results: Sean Yates finished fifth, Andy Hampsten eighteenth, Kiefel thirty-third, and Gerhard Zadrobilek sixty-first.

LeMond preferred to dwell on his personal triumph rather than a mechanical one, and in point of fact his willpower, returning form, and zest for victory meant more than the handlebars. It was neither the bars nor a miracle, both of which he credited, as much as the fact that when he had his body under control he was one of the best cyclists of his time. He had proven it as an amateur, then as a professional, and now that he was winning again he began thinking like a winner. With the yellow jersey on his back, he felt stronger, more sure of himself, he said.

Not that the race was over yet. In fact, it had really just begun, and LeMond pointed out that the two riders he feared most, Pedro Delgado and Laurent Fignon, had finished second and third behind him. The Spaniard had climbed back from 198th place to 28th, less than seven minutes behind LeMond; nevertheless, it was still easy to dismiss Delgado's chances, as Fignon did. "I can see him in the first five when the race ends, maybe even in the first three, but it's impossible for him to make up seven minutes and win," the Frenchman said. "Even two minutes will be hard. Delgado is in an impossible situation. If he goes all out and attacks one day and gains five minutes, he'll be committing suicide because he'll have to collapse. And if he goes around trying to snatch thirty seconds here, thirty seconds there, he won't be able to get enough of them." What would Fignon do in his place? "I'm not in his place," he answered coldly. Which was certainly true; he was in second place overall, only five seconds behind LeMond.

For most of the next week the two kept their respective positions as the Tour completed its march along the flat to the

Pyrenees. On the first day in the mountains, Delgado gained nearly thirty seconds on LeMond, and on the second day, three minutes and twenty-six seconds, which vaulted him into fourth place. But the man in the yellow jersey after the second day was no longer LeMond. Fignon gained the honor on the climb to Superbagnères as he attacked from a big group with only five hundred meters to go. LeMond immediately caught him and then suddenly began to wobble. Before he righted himself, Fignon had gained twelve seconds and was across the finish line, the new leader by 7 seconds.

"I made a mistake in trying to catch him too fast," LeMond admitted. He was free to talk after the race because the finish was at the crest of a mountain, and the roads down were closed until the last rider struggled up to the finish. "I tried to bluff him by getting right back on his wheel so that he'd think he'd never be able to get away, but I blew up."

The day was a folkfest, as race days in the Pyrenees and Alps usually are. On the flat, a fan usually sees the Tour whir past in a buzz of wheels and a small storm of dust. In the mountains, however, the riders fall into small groups as they labor slowly upward, and the race can take an hour to pass a given point. Fans know this, of course, and arrive early in the mountains to claim a site with a good view and to spend a substantial part of the day. On the climb to the Tourmalet pass, for example, Mr. and Mrs. Jean-Pierre Brachet and their three children— Loic, eight, Vincent, five, and Stephanie, four—were perched halfway up the mountain, staring down into the valley where fleecy clouds cast long shadows. "We're on vacation," said Brachet, a policeman in Bordeaux, who explained that he was not really a fan of bicycle racing. "I'll watch it on television sometimes, but no more than that. The Tour is different, though." Just then the race turned a curve far below and came into sight. Most conversation ceased for the next hour, until the last man in the pack had struggled by.

In the town of St.-Sauveur, Dr. Marie-José Gril had closed her office at eleven A.M. to watch the race pass and toast the riders with a few friends. They stood drinking white wine and lifting their paper cups as the Tour rolled through on its way to the next fearsome climb. Dr. Gril, who specializes in internal disorders, draws her patients from the people who come to St.-Sauveur to drink its mineral water at the spring just down the road from her office. "Next year we'll have a real party," she told a couple of visitors. "Promise you'll be here." A solemn oath was made.

Waiting to welcome the pack atop the Aspin pass was Raymond Cochet, an industrial designer from Pau. From a distance he could be mistaken for Fignon, right down to the granny glasses, ponytail, and Super U jersey, shorts, and cap. Up close, Cochet looked more his forty-four years than Fignon's twenty-nine. "Fooled you though, didn't I?" he asked jovially. He had been going to races for four years, hoping to chat with his idol. "It's never happened," he admitted. "Either he goes by too fast or he doesn't see me. We've never met, but I'll keep trying."

Cochet denied that he was the Fignon lookalike who, complete with the correct number pinned on his jersey, sneaked into the 1987 Tour as it crossed from West Germany into France and rode across the daily stage's finish line. "You mean there's another one like me?" he asked in wonder.

Fignon had claimed the yellow jersey on the tenth stage and lost it back to LeMond on the fifteenth, when the American used the triathlon handlebars again in another time trial and finished fifth, 47 seconds faster than the Frenchman, who fell back to second place, 40 seconds behind. "The bars weren't a factor today," said LeMond, because the course was uphill, where a rider is forced out of his tuck to find climbing power by standing on the pedals. LeMond spent the next day, a day off, with his wife, mother, and father, all of whom had joined him for the remainder of the Tour.

When the racing resumed, he showed the benefits of the rest. Attacked time and again on a demanding twenty-kilometer climb on the road from Gap to Briançon, he refused to yield, surging after each opponent, catching him, and then settling back into his climbing rhythm. At the end of the day he finished fourth but lost no time to any other leader, and even picked up thirteen seconds on Fignon. "I followed every attack today," LeMond said proudly at the finish. "The one I was really worried about was Delgado, and I never let him get away." Knowing that attrition had reduced LeMond's nine-man team to five besides himself, Delgado was the first to attack. After the American fought back, Raul Alcala of PDM, then Charly Mottet of RMO, and finally Gert-Jan Theunisse of PDM all shot off ahead of him. At each attack, the others sat back and forced the isolated American to do the heavy work of regaining lost ground. Near the top of the climb, Mottet tried again before Delgado opened a fifty-meter lead, the biggest of the day. Once again LeMond drew even just before the group passed over the top and began the long descent to Briançon. Turning on the steam as the riders hit speeds of up to sixty miles an hour, LeMond led the descent.

"Delgado was able to get back to me at the finish," LeMond said. "He's a very strong rider and is the only one here to worry about, I think. That's if I have another good day tomorrow. If I do—if I come out of tomorrow's stage a little ahead or even a little behind—I'd say I was in a strong position to win." For the first time LeMond was allowing himself to say what would have been unspeakable just two weeks before.

Fignon was also on LeMond's mind. "With nearly a minute's lead over him, I have to hope that he'll feel he has to answer every attack tomorrow. I'll be watching everybody, especially Delgado, but some of the others have to share the load now." If he seemed to underestimate Fignon, LeMond knew that Delgado always rode well in the mountains but that the Frenchman inevitably cracked there. Not since he won the 1984 Tour had Fignon gotten over both the Alps and Pyrenees without a huge loss of time.

The next morning, just before the start of the dreaded climb to Alpe d'Huez in the toughest mountain stage of them all, LeMond was still confident. "I feel strong, stronger even than yesterday," he said. Then he stared out at the mountains surrounding the city of Briançon, and his face grew troubled. "But you never know until you get up into the hills how strong you are."

Five hours later LeMond knew. He had been strong, but not quite strong enough in the last four kilometers to keep the yellow jersey. Finishing fifth, he slipped back to second place overall, twenty-six seconds behind Fignon, who had also gained the yellow jersey at Alpe d'Huez in both of his victorious Tours, and who had openly predicted that this race would once again be decided there.

"I did my best," LeMond said, "and the race is far from being over." In his hotel he was keeping a private appointment he had made that morning. Disappointed and weary after two and a half weeks of racing, he had refused to give any other interviews that evening, but kept his word for a commitment already made. Fresh from the shower, he was still toweling himself off as he tried to hide his obvious disappointment. "I really can't complain. I truly had no idea I was going to ride this well. I had some hopes of winning a stage, and maybe of a top-twenty finish. I was really going to be happy with that. But of course now I want it all. This has been a very successful Tour for me. Even if I'm second, it's as big an achievement as my winning in '86. Maybe even bigger. When you have three, four, or five years to work yourself into victory, it's one thing, but to suddenly turn yourself around . . ." He left the sentence unfinished.

LeMond thought he knew what had gone wrong on the climb to Alpe d'Huez. "Maybe I put too much effort into yesterday's stage and paid at the end today. I felt good all day, but I had a moment there when they attacked—one kilometer—and then I had to recuperate for another kilometer. Just two bad kilometers out of all that we rode today. I felt better toward the end, but that's bike racing." He laughed mournfully.

LeMond took comfort from his overall performance, comparing it favorably to his Tour form in 1984 and 1985, when he finished third and second respectively. "But I was riding a little stronger in the hills in 1986," he admitted. "Each time I've lost time I've been wearing the yellow jersey. Fignon has yet to be wearing it at a crucial moment. He's had it through some easy stages and lost it in the time trial. It takes a lot of effort and responsibility when you've got it."

But wasn't the yellow jersey an advantage to a rider, endowing him with strength? "I think it's more a disadvantage when you're going through the mountains," LeMond answered. "You're left alone. Everybody can take it easy and expect you to do the work. I'm happy to have it, but it takes a lot of energy. You're extremely nervous when you have the yellow jersey. It changes you."

He was planning to ride more cautiously during the rest of the way to Paris, LeMond said. "If there's an opportunity to make up time, I'll take it, but I'm not going to attack all day and end up running out of steam in the last two kilometers. Now Fignon has the responsibility of controlling the race—and not just me, but Delgado too. He's definitely still in it."

How did LeMond like the Frenchman? Their rivalry was

long-standing and sometimes even personal, but they had known each other for many years, starting when they were both youngsters with the Renault team.

"I liked him more before this Tour," LeMond responded. "I still like him, but he's a guy easier to like when he's not winning. When he is—and I saw it in '84—he completely changes. That's normal because of the pressure, but I prefer people who are the same, win or lose. It's hard to be nice to everybody in the Tour, sign autographs, give interviews. You really don't have the energy, and a lot of people don't understand that."

Looking slowly around the room, LeMond tried to sum up his feelings. "I have a lot of respect for Fignon because he's a very good rider," he said finally. "He's determined, and he's gone through a few bad years, too. It's nice to see him riding well again. I just wish he wasn't riding *this* well." He burst out laughing.

The next morning, as he awaited the whistle calling riders to the starting line, Fignon returned the compliment. "I have a lot of respect for him too," he said of LeMond. "I know how much work you have to do to get back to the top, and I'm glad he made it. I'm glad I did, too."

Fignon confirmed reports that he realized LeMond had weakened on the climb because of his body language. From years of riding together, the Frenchman knew that when LeMond started rocking slightly forward and backward as he climbed, it meant that he was weary. His Super U coach, Cyrille Guimard, had noticed the telltale sign too and had drawn up to Fignon in the team car, and they had decided to attack with four kilometers to go. At exactly that point, marked by a yellow banner over the road, Fignon jumped ahead and opened a lead of one hundred meters. Delgado went after him immediately, but LeMond could only watch as Fignon opened a bigger and bigger gap on his way to the yellow jersey.

Now the French rider and coach were sitting in the shade of a tent at the foot of Alpe d'Huez, Guimard holding court as Fignon read an account in a French paper relating how he had reclaimed the jersey with his strong climb. "The Heights of Glory," the article was headlined, and Fignon read it with grave attention. Signing autographs desultorily without looking at his fans, he was in a typically prickly mood. When a woman asked him to smile for a photograph, he snarled, "Smile, smile. I'm just as cute when I don't smile."

Not to the public, he wasn't. Earlier in the spring Fignon had been deliberately rude to photographers during the Giro d'Italia, turning his back whenever they appeared. There was something comical about the photographers' complaint that they had more pictures of his ponytail than of his face. He had continued this boycott during the Tour, so in addition to the yellow jersey he had just won another prize, the Prix Citron, or Lemon Prize, awarded by press photographers to the least courteous rider. The balloting had not even been close; Fignon took thirty-five of the thirty-seven votes, with Eric Vanderaerden, a Belgian, his only challenger.

The French public appeared to be just as repelled by Fignon, regarding as arrogance what he thought of as being cool. Few signs encouraging him appeared on the side of the Tour's roads, and the cheers for him at each finish were feeble. It hadn't helped earlier in the season when a French bicycling magazine asked him about complaints by his teammates that they hardly knew him. His reply had been brusque: "They're paid to ride for me, not to become my friends."

Yet Fignon had supporters who tried to explain his aloofness. "He concentrates so hard that he forgets about a lot of other things," said a former teammate, Jean-René Bernaudeau. "Even his wife says that he's unbearable when he's concentrating the way he is now."

Bernard Hinault, who was not always the people's choice either, had his own answer to the question of whether the public was for or against Fignon. "Like always, some are for him, some against—that's the French public," Hinault grumbled. "Each of us has his own character. I think he's come to win the Tour, and that's what he's trying to do, not make friends. His will to win is driving him."

On this day Fignon went out and showed how accurate Hinault's analysis was. Surprising the rest of the pack by attacking on what was expected to be a quiet stage after the ordeal of Alpe d'Huez, Fignon bounded away on a short climb to the resort of Villard de Lans. Racing past meadows brown with the stubble of fresh-cut hay and mountains hazy in the heat, he ended up winning by 24 seconds. When he crossed the finish line, he thrust his arms upward twice before punching the air with his fist.

A few minutes later, Fignon awarded victory kisses to women on the winner's podium. "The race isn't over yet," he announced to an unbelieving audience, "but I helped myself today by looking for an opportunity and making the most of it." LeMond now trailed by 50 seconds and Delgado, who had lost 33 seconds, by 2 minutes and 28 seconds. With only three stages to go, the Spaniard was at last out of the running for a second successive victory.

In what seemed then like a last hurrah, LeMond reclaimed some glory the next day by winning the stage to Aix-les-Bains in a sprint finish over Fignon. The stage, over the last of the Alps, amounted to a duel among the first four leaders, each hoping to see the others crack and fall behind. None did, and the "royal breakaway" group of LeMond, Fignon, Delgado, Theunisse, and Marino Lejarreta finished together more than two minutes ahead of the pack.

The final stage before the time trial from Versailles to Paris was on the flat and there was no hope of a breakaway, so LeMond knew that his only chance lay on the last day. "I'm glad to see the end of the mountains," he said. "I haven't been riding very well there for the last few days. I congratulate Laurent Fignon for what he's done. He's been very strong in climbing, but I think I'm a little better on the flat."

With a fifty-second deficit, LeMond knew that "a little better" would not be enough in the time trial. "It's going to be difficult, but I think it's still possible to win," he insisted.

There were few believers. The time trial would be less than twenty-five kilometers long, and to make up two seconds a kilometer seemed impossible.

16

"Unbelievable, Just Unbelievable"

The night before the final time trial, reporters asked Paul Koechli if Greg LeMond could possibly make up fifty seconds. As the former manager of La Vie Claire, Koechli knows LeMond and his abilities well. In addition, he is regarded as one of the finer minds in the sport, a master at training and strategy, a devotee of the computer in assessing a rider's performance. Koechli is also extremely fond of LeMond personally, which would have tended to affect his judgment. "It's not possible," he said nevertheless. "One second a kilometer is possible. Two seconds a kilometer is impossible."

"I THOUGHT IT was possible to win," Greg LeMond insisted weeks later. "I thought it was possible," he repeated, "but it was a lot of time to make up."

He felt strong that Sunday in Versailles as a huge crowd lined the starting area on the Avenue de Paris to watch the

138 remaining riders in the Tour de France begin the time trial, a little over 24.5 kilometers (fifteen miles) to the finish on the Champs-Elysées.

The day started overcast before the summer sun burned the clouds off and left the sky a washed blue. By midafternoon the temperature was in the low eighties, hot for Paris, with a light wind tempering the heat. LeMond had slept well, eaten a big breakfast and lunch, and gone for a long warm-up ride; he was feeling confident. As he neared the start, many spectators yelled encouragement. He seemed not to hear them, except that every now and again he would smile back at a fan who shouted at him. Everything depended on this time trial, but the atmosphere was joyful, not tense. It was a Sunday in July, a holiday, the last weekend before August, when Parisians traditionally depart on their month-long vacation.

Not since 1975 had the Tour de France ended with a time trial. Since that year, the surviving riders had entered Paris in a pack, made six passes up and down the Champs-Elysées, and then sprinted wildly toward the final finish line. When the course had been announced in October 1988, no one would have guessed that the last stage would decide the race, but nearly everybody approved of the return to a final time trial. "It's fine being sucked along on a free ride down the Champs-Elysées," said Andy Hampsten, the 7-Eleven leader. "The greatest moment of the Tour always is arriving on the Champs-Elysées, just finishing the race. But arriving alone and not having to share the cheers is a wonderful reward for everybody."

Indeed, there would be cheers for every rider, though interest centered on only two of them. No tie was possible because the stage would be timed down to hundredths of a second. If this failed to resolve a tie, the riders' placings in all twenty-one previous stages would be added. Finally, if even that produced a stalemate, the race would be decided by the outcome of the previous day's stage: LeMond 40th, Fignon 50th as the riders skylarked in the traditional easy stage just before the Tour ended. But nobody believed that any tie-breakers would be needed, and virtually no one thought that LeMond could overcome his deficit.

The American would leave at 4:12 in the afternoon and Fignon at 4:14. They would be the last two off, since in a time trial riders start in inverse order of standing. Those far behind in the rankings had left a minute apart, but the leading twenty riders started two minutes apart.

With a 50-second lead, Fignon should have been feeling fine that morning, but he wasn't. When the riders had reached Paris by train the evening before, French television showed Fignon spitting at the cameras, striding away angrily from all questioners and appearing even more irritable than usual. "You want a punch in the mouth?" he asked one cameraman. A few days before, he said later, he had begun to be troubled by saddle sores that had quickly infected his urinary system. On the next-to-last stage he had been unsure that he could even finish, so great was the discomfort. Unable to sit comfortably on the narrow saddle, he had to cut short his warm-up for the final time trial because of the pain. He could not take any painkillers or most other medicine, of course, because of the long list of drugs forbidden as performance enhancers.

In contrast, LeMond was feeling good. The evening before, French television had showed him smiling and relaxed, quite willing to chat with reporters on the train entering Paris. The contrast with Fignon's rude behavior was striking.

The American's confidence carried over to the next morning. After finishing his warm-up ride, LeMond was sure he would do well. A month later he recalled the feeling as he rested on a trainer's table while Otto Jácome kneaded his legs after a training session for the world championship road race in the Savoy region of France. Lying on his stomach with a towel knotted around his waist and a faraway look in his eyes, LeMond recalled the last morning of the Tour de France. "I told Otto, 'My legs are good. I'm going to have a very good day.'" Jácome nodded, remembering that morning too. Suddenly they were both far from the small, shabby hotel room in Aix-les-Bains and back in Versailles, with the royal palace as a backdrop to the Tour's simple platform and starting ramp.

"That Giro time trial was the race that turned things around," LeMond was saying. "It gave me a lot more confidence, and it changed the way I raced time trials. I'd kind of forgotten how to do them. That day in Italy I decided to go all out from the beginning, and if I ran out of gas with five kilometers to go, at least I could say that I'd pushed myself to the max. I did it that day and wound up getting second. I was shocked; I'd thought that maybe I'd be in the top ten."

On the platform in Versailles, covered with a canopy against the hot July sun, LeMond reached down one last time to ritually check the shoes locked into his bicycle pedals. A clock showed that he would leave within seconds.

"Five," announced the timer in French.

"I was nervous," LeMond admitted.

"Four."

"I don't like doing time trials."

"Three."

"When I'm warming up, I say to myself, 'I don't know if I can do this again.'"

"Two."

"You think, 'Oh my God, I've got to push myself to the limit for the next thirty minutes, or however long it is.'"

"One."

"But when I finish one, I've always liked it. I excel at them."

Then LeMond was rolling down the ramp, surging for 26 minutes and 57 seconds through Viroflay, Chaville, Sèvres, Meudon, and many of the other southwestern suburbs of

Paris. "I started extremely fast," he remembered. In a time trial a rider can judge how he is doing by how quickly he catches the rider who left before him—or how quickly he himself is caught by the rider who departs after him. Team managers driving behind the rider can shout out his time at different points in the course, but for this last stage LeMond did not want to know. After the ADR coach gave him his time at the five-kilometer sign, LeMond told him he didn't want any further information. Instead he emptied his head of all thought except riding as fast as he could. "I didn't think; I just rode," was the way he put it. His strategy was an easy one since he had nothing to lose by going flat out from start to finish. He laughed lightly in recollection. "It was pretty simple, really."

Wearing an aerodynamic helmet and leaning on the Scott extensions on his handlebars, LeMond rode with his back bent and his head low but often bobbing. When he passed the Arc de Triomphe and turned down the Champs-Elysées with the finish in sight, he appeared to reach back and find the strength for one more long kick. "I rode as if my whole career depended on it," he said. "I knew that at the finish my whole family would be waiting for me."

So strongly did LeMond ride that when he crossed the finish line he did not even feel spent. "It was weird. I felt I'd put less effort . . ." he began. "No, I put an all-out effort . . ." Again he broke off. "I almost felt when I crossed the line that I hadn't pushed myself enough." In fact, he went on, he felt that he could have ridden at the same pace for another ten miles.

Then there began the wait for Fignon to finish. Standing in the middle of the Champs-Elysées in a crush of reporters, photographers, and race officials, the American watched the Frenchman moving toward the Arc de Triomphe. Loudspeakers boomed out his time and an electronic clock near LeMond showed the widening deficit. Starting fast, Fignon had been so startled to hear his coach, Cyrille Guimard, shout at the five-kilometer mark that already he trailed LeMond by six seconds that he had stopped pedaling for a moment and turned in astonishment to look at his team car. After 11.5 kilometers of the 24.5, LeMond led Fignon by 21 seconds and the gap kept rising; it was 24 seconds after fourteen kilometers, 35 seconds after eighteen kilometers, and 45 seconds after twenty kilometers, when Fignon turned left at the Louvre and entered the Rue de Rivoli, then the Place de la Concorde, and at last the Champs-Elysées.

Now the Frenchman shifted gears and began his descent away from the Arc de Triomphe. "All I could think of was how terrible it would be to lose by one second," LeMond remembered.

Fignon was still about fifty meters from the finish line when he lost the race. At that point the clock showed that he trailed LeMond by 50 seconds for the day and that their times for the full 2,025 miles of the Tour de France were equal—but he still had fifty meters to ride.

While LeMond watched the final seconds, French television reporters gave him a set of earphones in an attempt to interview him, but the crowd noise prevented him from hearing their questions and from getting any information about his rival's time. Then, as it became clear that Fignon would not finish in time, LeMond began pumping the air with his fists, broke into a huge grin, and punched one uppercut after another. Standing near him and holding his bicycle, Jácome suddenly shouted, "You won it, Greg, you won it," as Fignon passed the line. Jácome let out a whoop and went bounding up the avenue in joy, dragging the bicycle behind him.

Kathy LeMond was in tears. As she heard Bernard Hinault announce the final time, she shouted at her husband, "Eight seconds, Greg. You've got eight seconds less than Fignon." LeMond heard her voice and understood only some of her words, but by that time he already knew the result.

"I didn't know I'd won it until Fignon crossed the line," he said. "You hear so many things at a moment like that. Some guy said Fignon had twenty seconds to make it to the finish, and he looked so close that I thought I'd lost. But then when he crossed the line I knew the time. From that point it was unbelievable, just unbelievable."

Almost lost in the turmoil was the fact that Fignon had not folded under pressure. He finished 58 seconds behind, good enough for third place on the day, but LeMond had won the stage and the Tour de France by 8 seconds.

After 2,025 miles, just 8 seconds, which was 30 fewer than the previous smallest margin in the race. In 1968, Jan Janssen, a Dutchman, had trailed Herman Van Springel, a Belgian, by 16 seconds and beat him by 54 in a time trial into Paris on the final day. LeMond's speed of 54.5 kilometers an hour (thirty-four miles an hour) was the fastest ever for a winner of a daily stage in the Tour de France, by nearly five kilometers an hour.

Gasping for breath and drinking a bottle of mineral water as he sprawled on the ground, Fignon at first offered no excuses for his defeat. "I rode the hardest I could," he said. "Obviously it wasn't good enough." Later he complained about his saddle sores. "I could hardly sit because it was so painful," he said. "I wasn't even sure I would be able to start today." Television replays of his ride showed him thrashing in the saddle and often leaning to the right. Strangely, Fignon had not given himself any aerodynamic advantages other than two disc wheels (to LeMond's one), refusing even to wear a helmet. He had been seen in Versailles with a crude set of triathlon handlebars that morning, but they had not been in place for the time trial. Much later, Guimard complained that

LeMond's bars should not have been allowed, saying that they had never been approved by the "correct" body of international officials. He might even sue, Guimard threatened.

As he recalled his time on the victory podium, LeMond did not refer to Fignon or Guimard. Again he was hearing half a million people cheering him, and again he remembered thinking that only a month and a half earlier he had been ready to quit cycling. "I thought about everything that happened the last two years—mainly the suffering, the Tour of Italy, and all the bad races. I was thinking about how fast my body turned around." None of his memories extended further back than the shooting. There was no reliving his time on the same podium three years earlier. "It never entered my mind."

All in all, LeMond continued, there were few things he would have done differently, except for the ADR team's victory celebration at a nightclub. "It was like an oven and I was so tired," he said. "If I ever do that again, I want to get one of those big boats on the Seine and have dinner on it and be cool."

Months later, Guimard was continuing his battle against the Scott handlebars. Fignon had tried to use them in a race in Belgium and was told that they were not yet authorized by the same International Cycling Union officials who had allowed LeMond and others to use them in the Tour. Guimard's protest seemed to cast doubt on the validity of LeMond's victory.

"The debate is absolutely ridiculous," LeMond said, his voice rising, when he was asked to comment. "Guimard's trying to create a problem either for publicity or to take away the value of my victory. In the Tour of Italy I used the same equipment as Fignon and beat him by almost two minutes. He hasn't beaten me in a time trial in four years, at least not in the ones where I've gone all out. In that last stage, you could say that the handlebars added one second, but you could also say that his front disc wheel added a second. They had a choice in equipment, and clearly they felt that the handlebars made no difference. I'd have no objection if the regulations said that no disc wheels or special handlebars could be used; then you'd have just the athlete. But as we know in cycling and car racing, equipment is very important. Why didn't Fignon wear a helmet? He knows that it takes off seconds. It was his decision. He was too confident." Or too bound to tradition, perhaps. Choice of equipment is not a science, as LeMond himself showed when he used a rear disc wheel instead of Fignon's two. He judged—inaccurately, as it happened—that the light wind would destabilize a bicycle with two disc wheels and offset any gain in speed.

"I think Guimard's reaction is very unsportsmanlike and shows that he's a bad loser. When you get second place, you say, 'I could have won it here, I could have won it there.' When you win, you never say anything; it's finished."

He was not criticizing Fignon, LeMond made clear, but Guimard, with whom his relationship has been troubled ever since he left the Renault team in late 1984. Toward Fignon he remained sympathetic. As he said after the victory ceremony, "When I saw him on the podium, what could I say to him? What could he say to me? I would have been devastated to lose by eight seconds."

Worse was to come for Fignon at the world championships late in August. "Superman!" shouted the headline across the front page of the French sports newspaper *L'Equipe*. "Fantastique Greg LeMond," replied the headlines across the front page of *The Dauphiné Libéré*, the local paper in Chambéry, where the championships were held.

LeMond had not taken long to answer the question "What do you do for an encore?" Barely a month after he won the Tour de France for the second time, he won the world championship road race for the second time. "It's really a great year," he said shortly after crossing the finish line in a four-man sprint. "I never would have believed this."

In point of fact, LeMond was being modest. For days beforehand, he had believed in the possibility of victory, and had said, "It's going to be a matter of whoever's strongest," even dropping a few hints that he was talking about himself.

"He says he feels good," explained Andy Bishop, another member of the twelve-man U.S. team. LeMond had invited Bishop to train with him in the Alps for two weeks beforehand. "We've made a lot of long rides in the mountains, up to six and a half hours a day," Bishop said before the race. "He's really been hammering. He's got a good chance to win, but he'll have to have a super day."

He did, and if anybody believed it, that person was Fignon, who had spent the whole summer measuring his career in seconds. First he lost the Tour de France by eight seconds, then won the Tour of Holland by one second over his teammate Thierry Marie, and finally finished three seconds behind LeMond, taking sixth place, in the world championships. Afterward the Frenchman summed it up wryly: "When I attacked on the last climb up the Montagnole Hill, who chased and caught me? LeMond. When I attacked again later, who counterattacked? LeMond. When I tried to get away with a kilometer to go, who came after me? LeMond. This has been LeMond's year, and he's really become my bête noire."

LeMond added a detail: "When I caught Fignon just at the start of the last kilometer, he made a gesture with his hand, as if he was saying, 'Some day you'll pay for this.' "

The prospect did not make LeMond tremble, since he was speaking after donning his new rainbow-striped jersey and was wearing a gold medal around his neck. He had earned both of them the old-fashioned way. After he had surveyed the 12.3-kilometer (7.55-mile) course that he and the rest of the

190-man field would have to ride twenty-one times, he pronounced it hard. "One of the toughest in a long time," he added. "That hill will take it out of everybody. Twenty-one times over that hill! Phew! And if it's hot!" He rolled his eyes at the prospect.

Luckily the previous week's blazing sun disappeared. By the time the race began, dark clouds covered the Alpine valley in which Chambéry sits, and the nearby mountain peaks were smudges. Four hours into the six-hour-and-forty-five-minute race, a cold, heavy rain started to fall. It continued for more than an hour and then drizzled intermittently until the finish.

On the eighth lap, nine riders attacked and built a lead of 4 minutes 50 seconds by the eleventh lap, at which point four of the group—Thomas Wegmuller of Switzerland, Thierry Claveyrolat of France, Alexei Konichev of the Soviet Union, and Martin Ducrot of the Netherlands—broke away again. By the nineteenth lap, Claveyrolat and Konichev had left the two others behind; although their lead was down to 1:28, there were only twenty-five kilometers left to race. Was the world championship going to be decided between the twenty-three-year-old Russian, whose major accomplishment heretofore had been a victory in the previous year's amateur Giro d'Italia, and the slight Frenchman, who is known as a good climber in minor races?

No, it was not. Deciding that his time had come, Steven Rooks of the Netherlands caught the twosome, and their lead was down to 11 seconds at the bell lap as LeMond and Fignon rode with seven others in pursuit. "I felt terrible the whole race until two laps to go," LeMond said. "I was ready to quit, but I figured a lot can happen in the last two laps." While the rain continued to pour down, Fignon attacked on the climb, was amazed to see LeMond suddenly back with him, attacked again, and was caught again. Then Sean Kelly of Ireland joined them, and together the three caught the leaders.

At the red triangle marking the final kilometer, Fignon tried for the last time to get away and was again countered by LeMond. With 200 meters to go, the American decided it was time to sprint. "I felt good and just went all out at the finish," he said. "I didn't want to be behind Kelly if he started sprinting because I knew I'd never catch him."

Fignon and Claveyrolat were left behind as the four others tore for the line. LeMond was the obvious winner by half a wheel and raised his right arm in triumph as he shot across the line. Konichev, who LeMond remembered had once beaten him in a sprint in the Coors Classic, was second, and a photograph was needed to decide that Kelly had nipped Rooks for the bronze medal. "Third place, second place—they're both meaningless," Kelly grumbled. "All that counts is first place."

LeMond could not have agreed more.

17

The Five-Million-Dollar Man

*All the dumb poses were requested again, though none was quite
as numbing as the one from the 1986 Tour victory: Greg and
Kathy LeMond in bed in their hotel under an American flag.
This time the American theme was limited to LeMond wearing the
robes and crown of the Statue of Liberty. Much was made yet
again of the fact that he was American, so unexpected a
nationality in a European sport. For one brief moment, to be
American was to have it all. Thus Jean-Luc Vandenbroucke, the
manager of Belgium's Lotto team, announced: "Greg's secret is the
American dream and his exceptional class. If the Americans have
been innovators in so many domains (medicine, sports, the
conquest of space, automobiles), they owe everything to their sense
of challenge. He had a goal and nothing could keep him from it."
For an instant, it was again the American Century.*

WITH THE JERSEY of the world champion on his back,
LeMond was again everybody's darling. He had nearly a

dozen criteriums to ride in France, and the crowds at each were huge. People were coming to see more than the winner of the Tour de France and the world championship; they were there to pay homage to the American who had triumphed over pain, suffering, and humiliation. "Welcome back from hell, Greg," said a magazine advertisement paid for by one of his many commercial sponsors.

LeMond had made a lot of money this season: his $500,000 salary, the $350,000 victory bonus that ADR owed him for winning the Tour de France and the world championship, a flood of new endorsements, the handful of criteriums after the Tour, and now the ten criteriums he had scheduled between the world championships and his return to Minnesota three weeks later. His asking price to appear in a criterium had been $10,000, and he honorably did not raise it once the rainbow-striped jersey was on his back; late offers, however, rose above $30,000.

That was nice money for an afternoon's racing, but LeMond was also busy negotiating a change in teams for more money than had ever been dreamed of in professional bicycling. He was readying his second salary revolution after the one in 1984 that called for a three-year, $1 million contract with La Vie Claire at a time when top salaries stopped at about $150,000. In a ripple effect, the next highest salaries in the sport had since mounted to the $750,000 or $800,000 report-edly paid to Stephen Roche, Sean Kelly, and Pedro Delgado. The minimum salary, which is what the majority of the world's professional riders make, had also risen, from about $7,000 to an average of $30,000.

In mid-September 1989, LeMond told a news conference in Paris that he would ride in 1990 for the Z team under a three-year contract worth a minimum of $5.5 million. Both he and his new employer, Roger Zannier, declined to say how much each year of the contract with the French-based team was worth. Asked if he would be making $2 million in the third year, LeMond said, "Probably." With a shy smile he added, "I'm embarrassed to say."

The announcement followed weeks of bidding, most of it public. After the Tour, nine teams were reported to have tried to hire LeMond away from ADR, for whom he refused to ride again. Though he had signed a two-year contract with the Belgian team, he made it clear that he would not honor the second year, charging that the team had abrogated the contract by being consistently late in its salary payments. By the time of the world championships, he said that he had narrowed the offers down to three teams: 7-Eleven, Toshiba, and a combined Coors-French team, which was commonly thought to be Z. "My instinct is to go with 7-Eleven," he said, refusing to confirm that the American team wanted him badly enough to offer more than $1 million a year, the first time that barrier had been breached. Conceding that it was "a good possibility" that he would accept, he revealed that Coors had made a generous offer too. "I prefer being on an American team," he added. "I'm American, and I want to race back there." His son Geoffrey would be starting kindergarten in Minnesota in September and, he said, "If I'm going to be racing in September and October for the rest of my career, I want to do it in North America."

However, there were problems with LeMond's riding for 7-Eleven. Many of its racers had grown up competing against him, and some bad blood remained from those years. A few of its riders also remembered how LeMond had sometimes commented sarcastically about their schedule, which called for a short stay in Europe in the spring before returning to the United States and preparing there for the Tour de France. "In the U.S. the racing is never hard enough to bring out the best in a rider," LeMond has said repeatedly.

One 7-Eleven rider who announced that he would be glad

to have LeMond as a teammate was Ron Kiefel. "I think it's about time he joined us," he said at the world championships. "The team has progressed. We've made our mistakes, but now we're stronger, and we have some things we can offer him in help and teamwork. But if it doesn't happen, it will be because it's a business decision. This is a big business now, and it's not quite as simple as we like to think."

The bidding took a new turn a week later when *L'Equipe* announced that LeMond had signed a preliminary accord with Z. A major consideration, the paper said, was that Z had agreed to compete on Team LeMond bicycles, the brand his father was selling in the U.S. "It's practically done," LeMond was quoted as saying in virtually the same words he had used about 7-Eleven. Toshiba then raised the ante again, 7-Eleven responded, and rumors about teams and terms proliferated. To end them, LeMond called a news conference in a hotel ballroom rented by the Z team.

Thus the identity of the team was settled, and only the price was still the object of rumors. The night before the press conference, a French television station reported that LeMond had agreed to a three-year contract worth more than $8 million. Not so, he said as he took his place at a table facing about fifty reporters and a rank of television cameras. With him sat Zannier and Roger Legeay, the Z coach. The American began with a feeble attempt at humor by announcing in French that he had signed with a team in Chile, but Zannier quickly brought the proceedings under control by saying how pleased he was that LeMond would join Z for $5.5 million.

LeMond emphasized that he had not accepted the highest offer, which rumor listed as 40 million francs (then $6 million) from Toshiba. "They offered quite a bit more money," he said. "Z made a very good offer, but I did not choose the team with the most money." He also noted that Legeay had been the only team coach to show any interest in him *before* he'd won the time trial from Dinard to Rennes. "I prefer to be with a French team because it will allow me to program my season best for the Tour de France," he said. "I carefully analyzed each team, and Z had the climbers I will need to help me win the Tour again."

Giving a few details about the contract, LeMond explained that payment was to be in dollars, not francs, that it could go higher since it called for victory bonuses for himself and his teammates, and that it did indeed specify that the Z riders would use Team LeMond bicycles. The entire contract payment was backed by a letter of credit from one of France's major banks, Crédit Lyonnais, he added. "It's a bank guarantee, and it's better to have it because then both of us are comfortable," he said of himself and Zannier.

The Frenchman emphasized that his chain of franchised stores was growing bigger in France and was moving into Belgium and Spain. "To make the name known," he explained, "you can't be second or third in a race; you need a winner." Praising LeMond as "a great champion," Zannier said he had been deeply moved when the racer mounted the victory podium in Paris with his son Geoffrey in his arms. "Just the right image for us," he pointed out. Even so, he added, he had no plans to enter the American market.

Then Legeay, the Z coach, outlined the team's goals for the next season. "We want to win the Tour de France, the World Cup, and the world championship," he said. "Greg can do these things."

LeMond said he expected no problems in getting out of the year remaining in his contract with ADR, whose sponsor, François Lambert, was threatening to sue him. "If he wants to go to trial, I'm willing." (In 1990 ADR did sue, and the matter is in litigation.) He expected no trouble, he continued, over the year remaining on his contract with Coors Light. He would ride occasionally for the American team in exhibitions and publicity races, but not in major American races like the Tour de Trump. "I was good for them this year and they were good for me," he said, "and they understand and accept the change."

Turning to the subject of the 7-Eleven team, LeMond said, "I feel bad about them because it's a very good team. It just didn't work out. There were some things they just couldn't guarantee. They tried to find another sponsor, but I couldn't depend on that. I wanted to be with a team where I knew there was no problem. We tried to work it out, but in the end Z was a better deal for me. I had to think of my career. You have responsibilities to everybody, but the most important part is to look out for yourself."

Then came the question that seemed to sum up the whole season, from the humiliation of the Tour de Trump to the pain of the Giro d'Italia, from the idea of quitting to the joy of standing again on the victory podiums of the Tour de France and the world championships. In those two months LeMond had traveled far from that hunting field in California. How did it feel to leave Europe for the year $5 million richer than when he had arrived the winter before? LeMond was asked.

"It feels pretty good," he allowed. As usual these days, he was grinning.

The money was wonderful, no question about that, but the year ended with even better rewards. In October, Kathy gave birth to their first daughter, who was named Simone. Greg and Kathy had wanted a daughter so badly that they vowed to keep having children until one was a girl.

In December LeMond was chosen by the newspaper *L'Equipe* as its "champion of champions" among all the world's athletes, becoming the first cyclist to win the award since it was originated in 1980. That was not unexpected in France, where cycling is second only to soccer in popularity, but then came the news that confirmed LeMond's status as a superstar in his own country: *Sports Illustrated* named him "Sportsman of the Year" and put his photograph on the cover. Here was the recognition that LeMond had dreamed of for so many years. Inside the magazine, a fourteen-page article retold the story of his comeback and concluded, "With his prime competitive years now upon him, Greg LeMond, Sportsman of the Year, is back on top of the heap."

Yes, LeMond was truly back. At the start of the 1990 season, friends noticed his heightened confidence while he experienced his usual slow start. "I keep saying I'm suffering and it's hurting, but overall I can't complain," he said after his return to Europe from the off-season. "I'm extremely happy. I'm enjoying myself."

There was no reason to worry, LeMond kept saying, especially to himself. His celebrity status in the United States cost him up to three weeks of vital training during the winter— "One thing led to another and I found myself overwhelmed, too much to do," he explained. Having lived it up, he now was painfully living it down. "I'm hurting on hills," he admitted during the eight-day Paris–Nice race, which ended with Le-Mond far down in the standings. "I'm not bad, I'm just bad on the hills."

He proved that a few hours later by finishing a minute behind the rest of his team during a long and hilly time trial in the outskirts of St. Etienne. Riding over 44.5 kilometers of barren countryside, he stayed with his Z teammates until the final long uphill ramp, where he was left behind. "It was hard, a little too hard for me," he said.

But panic? "No, no, no," he said hurriedly when asked if he was worried about his poor showings in races in Spain and France during February and March. "Last year if I was riding this way or if I got dropped on a hill, I'd worry and get thinking whether there was something wrong with me. Now

I know nothing's wrong. It's just a matter of getting the kilometers in my legs. I should be fine by May or June.

"Next year—each year I say 'next year'—I want to train well in January and be in good shape when the season starts. But it never happens.

"Cycling has changed so much and everybody wants results so soon," he continued. "Everybody would like to see the world champion racing really well from February on, but my responsibility is to race really well in the Tour de France. As usual, that's my main goal."

Outside the hotel where he spoke it was still winter, but already his mind was concentrated on that one race of summer that all cyclists dream about winning. When it came time for the Tour de France, Greg LeMond would be riding for victory. He was on top again and intending to stay there.

ABOUT THE AUTHOR

SAMUEL ABT, a deputy editor of *The International Herald Tribune* in Paris, has written about the Tour de France for that newspaper and for *The New York Times* since 1977. Before he moved to France in 1971, he was a copy-editor for several newspapers in New England, for the *Baltimore Sun,* and for *The New York Times*. A graduate of Brown University, he has also been a Professional Journalism Fellow at Stanford University.